Our Language - An O...

You hear English spoken all day and see it in print everywhere, so you probably take it for granted. It just IS, like air and water, ever present and never changing.

But have you noticed that almost everything changes? Sometimes, change seems to be the only constant! Clothing and hair styles, music, cars, computer technology—always changing. The same goes for the language you speak. Over time, words come and go as they are needed, pronunciations change, definitions change, spellings change. Think about how many words you use that you never hear your parents use. Some of those words will be in future dictionaries, so you are yourself responsible for some of the changes we are referring to.

Lots of forces cause all these changes, but there was one big force that once changed the English language in a massive and magnificent way. It was an invasion a long time ago by an army that conquered the English people and changed the way they lived and spoke.

Let's go back in time almost a thousand years, to the early part of 1066, in England. If you heard someone speaking English then, you would hardly believe it was English. Here's an example of what you might have heared in a church:

> Þu ure fæder, þe eart on heofonum: Sy þin nama gehalgod. Cume ðin riċe. Sy ðin wylla on eorðan swaswa on heofonum. Syle us to dæg urne daghwamlican hlaf, ond forgyf us ure gyltas swaswa we forgyfað ðam þe wið us agyltað. Ond ne læd þu na us on costnunge, ac alys us fram yfele. Sy hit swa.

You can recognize a few words here and there, but on the whole, it's more like a foreign language than English, isn't it?

Then came the most significant event in the history of our language. In October of the year 1066, an army from across the channel that divides England from France stormed in and took control of the country. This army spoke a Latin-based language with a bit of Norse mixed in, a language called Norman French, and the new leaders demanded that from that time on, all business, all education, all worship, all writing be in their language, and the local native language was forbidden in public affairs.

Imagine being forced to learn a foreign language in order to carry on your life in your own homeland!

Thanks to the Battle of Hastings, the words of the winning Normans make up nearly 70% of the words found in our written texts

The English people, especially the younger ones, did indeed learn the Norman French language, but they didn't forget their old mother tongue. Privately, at home, they continued to speak their English, but in public, they obeyed the rules and spoke the victorious language. Over the years, what do you think happened? The people began to mix both languages together, using their native words in certain situations, and their new language in other situations, so much so that the mixture became one new language. Today that is English. This new English still has a double personality, with some words, the original English, being used in everyday speech, and the Latin-based version of those same words being used in writing and formal speech. That is why we have in English today two ways to express nearly everything: beside the word 'teacher', for example, we have "educator". With "motherly" we have "maternal"; with "car" we have automobile", and so on in thousands of examples. It is no exaggeration to say that modern English is a bilingual language.

The Bayeux Tapestry is the most important relic to survive from the 11th century. Who do you think commissioned this stitched chronicle of the Battle of Hastings

Harold, King of England, was killed by the invading Normans at the Battle of Hastings.

As it turns out, the words of the winning Normans still make up nearly 70% of the words found in written texts, in law, in medicine, in government—in all academic and formal English like that you see in your school textbooks. And so, just as the English speakers nearly a thousand years ago had to learn the "winning" words in order to succeed, so do we even today. The good news is that learning these winning words is not so hard—and is even fun—once you see how they work, how they are made up of pieces of meaning, called morphemes, used over and over in different combinations that build new words.

This vocabulary program is called WORDBUILD because it focuses on how words are built. The building blocks of words are actually pieces of meaning. The goal of the program is that you will never see a new word again without asking yourself what you already know about it.

Here is a formula to keep in mind:

W O R D = (prefix) + root + (suffix)

The parentheses are to show that those parts don't have to be used. All every word really needs is a root. The root is the core meaning of a word.

Figuring out the meanings of words is like solving a problem. In solving this problem, first find the root of the word. Sometimes the root is a word by itself, but most roots must have a prefix or suffix added to them to make words. Either way, the root of a word will be its core meaning. Prefixes and suffixes also have meaning. To figure out what a word means, look for any part whose meaning is familiar. When the meanings of these parts are added together, the underlying meaning of the word will begin to appear.

Root Squares

How many words can you make?

Start in any square. Your goal is to combine two or more word parts to make as many words in the 'form' family as you can. Write each word and the definition you can think of for it in the space provided at the bottom of the page. Use the back of the page if you need to.

uni	ed	al
ing	form	trans
in	at	ion

_____

_____

_____

_____

_____

_____

_____

_____

_____

_____

_____

Magic Squares

Select the best answer for each of the words in the 'form' family from the numbered definitions. Put the number in the proper space in the Magic Square box. If the total of the numbers is the same both across and down, you have found the magic number!

'form' means shape, appearance, or arrangement

WORDS	DEFINITIONS
A. transforming	1. to become similar in shape to something else; to comply
B. informational	2. condition of having one shape or appearance
C. uniformity	3. puts into accepted arrangement or shape
D. uniformed	4. attired in apparel of one shape or appearance
E. informative	5. shapes, appearances, or arrangements
F. transformation	6. act of moving across to another shape
G. formations	7. relating to providing shape to data
H. formalizes	8. serving to provide shape to data
I. formless	9. moving across to another shape or appearance
	10. having no shape

Magic Square Box

A.	B.	C.
D.	**E.**	**F.**
G.	**H.**	**I.**

Magic Number _____

www.dynamicliteracy.com

Stair Steps

Name

Fill in the missing letters of each 'form' word by using the definitions below
'form' means shape, appearance, or arrangement

1. | f | o | r | m | |
2. | f | o | r | m | |
3. | | | f | o | r | m | |
4. | | | | f | o | r | m |
5. | | | f | o | r | m | |
6. | | | | | f | o | r | m |
7. | f | o | r | m |
8. | | | f | o | r | m |
9. | | | | | f | o | r | m |

1. shapes, appearances, or arrangements
2. in accord with accepted shape or arrangement
3. gives shape to ideas
4. having one shape or appearance
5. without shape or arrangement; relaxed
6. to move across to another shape or appearance
7. shapes, appearances, or arrangements
8. knowledge arranged or shaped to be understood
9. devices that move across to another shape

The Class Trip to the Caverns

The school class took a trip to the caverns and received an education about the earth, without textbook or in the usual classroom arrangement. The change in appearance of the landscape as we crossed from the green and bright surface of the earth into the totally dark cavern was amazing. When the tour guide Rocky turned on the lights, we gasped to see the all the rock shapes and arrangements.

Some rock arrangements were shaped like eggs, and others were shaped like columns. Some of the columns had not yet met in the middle, and Rocky arranged information in our heads that these had names depending on whether they were growing down from the ceiling or up from the ground. Appearing to grow up from the ground were stalagmites all of one shape. Rocky said that the length of the stalactites hanging from the ceiling gives us well-arranged ideas about the age of the caverns. Still in their shaping and developing stage, the stalactites and stalagmites are millions of years old.

Some rock patterns that seemed badly shaped were a result of earthquakes. The earth changes its shape again and again itself every so often violently through volcanic eruptions and earthquakes. The trip served to shape data in our minds and we are eager to go one day to see other caverns.

Fill in the blanks below using words from the "form" family.

1. Without texts and classroom, the class got an _____ lesson on geology.

2. We were amazed at the _____ between the surface and the underground.

3. There are so many different types of rock _____ in the caverns.

4. The _____ rocks looked exactly like eggs.

5. The guide _____ us about how stalactites and stalagmites differ.

6. The stalagmites we saw were _____, all about two feet high.

7. The length of the stalactites gives us _____ about the age of the cavern.

8. Always changing its appearance, the earth is still in its _____ stage.

9. Where rock patterns seemed _____, we saw evidence of earthquakes.

10. Earthquakes and volcanoes _____ the landscape below and above the surface.

11. Our trip to the caverns was highly _____; we learned a lot about the earth.

Word Bank

conformation	informal	informed	transform
formations	information	malformed	transformation
formative	informative	oviform	uniformal

Morpheme Mania

Prefixes

con de trans uni

counter

Suffixes

ing ion at ive

form
shape, appearance, or arrangement

Words & Definitions

conform – to become similar in shape

Synonyms

agree

Antonyms

differ

Roots

Other

Build as many words as you can for this root family. Use the prefixes and suffixes listed, or add your own. If you use any "combining roots", add them to the "Other Roots" box. Try to think of an antonym and a synonym for each word you build.

www.DynamicLiteracy.com

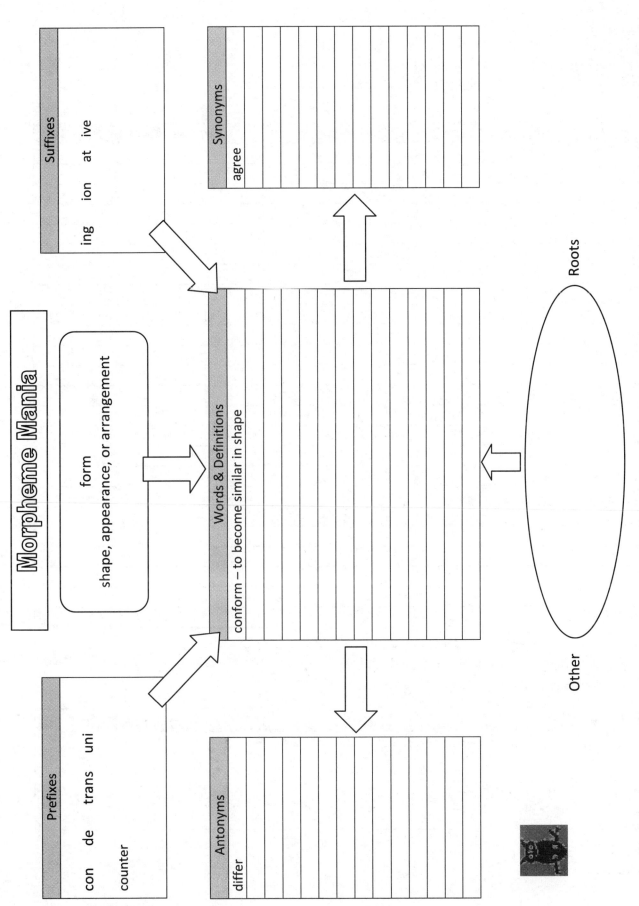

My Word Wall

Root: *form*

Word	Synonym / Antonym	Word	Synonym / Antonym

Morphemes for this meaning family

Prefixes	Roots	Suffixes

www.dynamicliteracy.com

Root Squares

Name

How many words can you make?

Start in any square. Your goal is to combine two or more word parts to make as many words in the 'pon, pone, pos, pose, post' family as you can. Write each word and the definition you can think of for it in the space provided at the bottom of the page. Use the back of the page if you need to.

com	er	de
ent	pon, pone, pos, pose, post	ite
post	ion	im

Magic Squares

Select the best answer for each of the words in the 'pon, pone, pos, pose, post' family from the numbered definitions. Put the number in the proper space in the Magic Square box. If the total of the numbers is the same both across and down, you have found the magic number!

'pon, pone, pos, pose, post' means to place, to put

WORDS	DEFINITIONS
A. opposition	1. act of being put out; act of being publicly shown
B. suppose	2. placement in conflict against
C. positive	3. items put together; units that make a whole
D. postponement	4. something put outside; a math symbol denoting the 'power' of numerical amount
E. exponent	5. people who put down; people who put money into a bank for safekeeping
F. disposers	6. the act of putting off until afterwards
G. imposition	7. certain of what is said or put forth; confident and sure of what is proposed
H. depositors	8. people who put away; people who throw things away after use
I. components	9. to put up; to offer up as a suggestion or argument
	10. the act of putting oneself in the way; the addition of a tax or task

Magic Square Box

A.	B.	C.
D.	E.	F.
G.	H.	I.

Magic Number ____

www.dynamicliteracy.com

Stair Steps

Name

Fill in the missing letters of each 'pon, pone, pos, pose, post' word by using the definitions below
'pon, pone, pos, pose, post' means to place, to put

1. | p | o | s | | |

2. | | | p | o | s | e |

3. | | | p | o | s | |

4. | | | | p | o | s | |

5. | | | | p | o | n | |

6. | | | p | o | n | |

7. | | | p | o | s | |

8. | | | | | | | p | o | s | e | |

9. | | | | | p | o | s | | | |

1. put on a deliberate manner or look; intentionally displayed a look or stance
2. to put in the way; to add on a tax or task
3. to put down; to put money into a bank for safekeeping
4. a person who puts together; a creator, especially of music
5. put off until afterwards
6. items put together; units that make a whole
7. quality of being placed in front; a part of speech placed in front of its object
8. puts down on top of something
9. act or process of leaving off from being put together; disintegration

www.dynamicliteracy.com

11

LOCAL LONER DISCOVERED TO BE MULTI-MILLIONAIRE

It was <u>put out</u> today that a local woman who died last week had been <u>putting herself forth</u> as a poor person but had <u>put down</u> millions every week over the years into the bank's place <u>for holding back accounts</u>. She left a will <u>to put away</u> all her wealth to her twenty first cousins. Penny N. Digent, who kept to herself, had held various <u>jobs</u> over the years and her neighbors had <u>put as a suggestion</u> that she had no relatives. The bank has <u>put forward an idea</u> that those who can prove their relationship with Ms. Digent should <u>put together</u> a family chart, with all the properly documented pieces put together, and bring it to the bank. People who <u>put themselves in a false light</u> will be arrested for fraud. The bank has <u>put off until later</u> setting a deadline for the charts.

Fill in the blanks below using words from the "pon, pone, pos, pose, post" family.

1. The bank's announcement _____ that the late Ms. Digent was a multi-millionaire.

2. Although very wealthy, she had been _____ as a poor person.

3. Every week she had _____ her money into the bank.

4. The bank had a special _____ for accounts like this one.

5. The bank wishes to _____ of this wealth as Ms. Digent wished.

6. Ms. Digent worked in several _____ over many years.

7. She never spoke of her relatives; _____ she had no family.

8. Official at the bank have _____ that qualifying relatives come forth.

9. Those qualified need to _____ a family tree.

10. This family tree must have all the legal _____ to document the relationship.

11. This way, the bank will be able to prevent _____ from getting the money.

12. A decision to set the deadline for the charts has been _____.

Word Bank

components	dispose	positions	proposed
compose	exposed	postponed	repository
deposited	impostors	posturing	supposedly

Morpheme Mania

Prefixes
re   ex   dis   de

com

Suffixes
ion   it   at   ive

Words & Definitions
positive – certain of what is put forth

pon, pone, pos, pose, post
to place or put

Synonyms
sure

Antonyms
negative

Roots

Other

Build as many words as you can for this root family. Use the prefixes and suffixes listed, or add your own. If you use any "combining roots", add them to the "Other Roots" box. Try to think of an antonym and a synonym for each word you build.

www.DynamicLiteracy.com

All rights reserved

13

Root: *pon, pone, pos, pose, post*

Word	Synonym / Antonym	Word	Synonym / Antonym

Morphemes for this meaning family

Prefixes	Roots	Suffixes

www.dynamicliteracy.com

Root Squares

Name

How many words can you make?

Start in any square. Your goal is to combine two or more word parts to make as many words in the 'quest, quis, quir, quire, quer' family as you can. Write each word and the definition you can think of for it in the space provided at the bottom of the page. Use the back of the page if you need to.

ac	ion	in
it	quest, quis, quir, quire, quer	con
ment	ive	re

Magic Squares

Select the best answer for each of the words in the 'quest, quis, quir, quire, quer' family from the numbered definitions. Put the number in the proper space in the Magic Square box. If the total of the numbers is the same both across and down, you have found the magic number!

'quest, quis, quir, quire, quer' means to ask, seek, gain

WORDS
A. acquires
B. requisitioner
C. questionably
D. conquerable
E. unquestionable
F. requirement
G. inquired
H. inquisitively
I. exquisite

DEFINITIONS
1. seeking into; searching for information
2. a person who formally seeks back; a person who demands as necessary
3. highly desirable to be sought out; superb
4. able to be gained completely; able to be defeated
5. sought into; searched for information
6. not subject to being asked about; definite or sure
7. in a manner subject to be asked about; uncertainly
8. something that must be sought back; something demanded as necessary
9. brings gain to; seeks and gains
10. in a manner tending seek into or ask; in a manner tending to question

Magic Square Box

A.	B.	C.
D.	E.	F.
G.	H.	I.

Magic Number ____

www.dynamicliteracy.com

Stair Steps

Name

Fill in the missing letters of each 'quest, quis, quir, quire, quer' word by using the definitions below
'quest, quis, quir, quire, quer' means to ask, seek, gain

1. | q | u | e | s | t | |
2. | | | q | u | e | s | t |
3. | | | q | u | i | r |
4. | | | | q | u | e | r |
5. | | | q | u | e | s | t |
6. | | | q | u | i | s |
7. | | | q | u | i | r | e |
8. | | | | | | q | u | e | r |

1. acts of seeking; missions or searches
2. to ask back; to call for or ask as a favor
3. brought gain to; sought and gained
4. a person who gains completely; a person who forcefully obtains power and control over
5. asking back; calling for or asking as a favor
6. tending to seek into or ask; tending to question
7. things that must be sought back; things demanded as necessary
8. not able to be gained completely; not able to be defeated

LOOK IT UP

Even if you don't have a suit of armor or a battle-steed, you can still go on a <u>search</u> for the Holy Grail, hidden gold mines, or even Faberge eggs. All you need to <u>seek and gain</u> the riches of the universe or to <u>obtain power and control over</u> uncharted lands or dragons is a thirst to <u>seek into things</u> and the special, <u>needed</u> ticket: your library card. Armed with burning <u>uncertainties</u> and a couple hours of free time, you could be with the climbers at their <u>complete gain</u> of Mt. Everest, or you could look over the shoulders of the commission during their <u>acts of seeking into</u> the assassination of an American president.

The next time your kid brother approaches you with a look <u>that tends to seek</u> in his eyes, amaze him with your understanding of water biomes or space explorers. Explore the universe with some good books!

<u>Fill in the blanks below using words from the "quest, quis, quir, quire, quer" family.</u>

1. Stories and movies about a _____ for rare items and adventure are exciting.

2. Through books you can _____ the riches of the universe.

3. In your reading you can _____ dragons.

4. A thirst to _____ into all kinds of subjects helps our minds grow.

5. A library card is a _____ ticket to access thousands of books.

6. It is good to ask yourself _____ and be curious.

7. Edmund Hillary made his _____ of Mt. Everest in 1953.

8. The Warren Commission made several _____ into the death of President Kennedy.

9. Little children and animals sometimes have an _____ look in their eyes.

<u>Word Bank</u>

acquire	inquire	quest	requirements
conquer	inquiries	questionable	requisite
conquest	inquisitive	questions	unconquered

Morpheme Mania

Prefixes

re   in   con   re

un

quest, quis, quir, quire, quer
to ask, seek, gain

Suffixes

ion   it   ment   ive

s   ed   able   er

Words & Definitions

questionable – subject to being asked about

Synonyms

unsure

Antonyms

certain

Roots

Other

Build as many words as you can for this root family. Use the prefixes and suffixes listed, or add your own. If you use any "combining roots", add them to the "Other Roots" box. Try to think of an antonym and a synonym for each word you build.

www.DynamicLiteracy.com

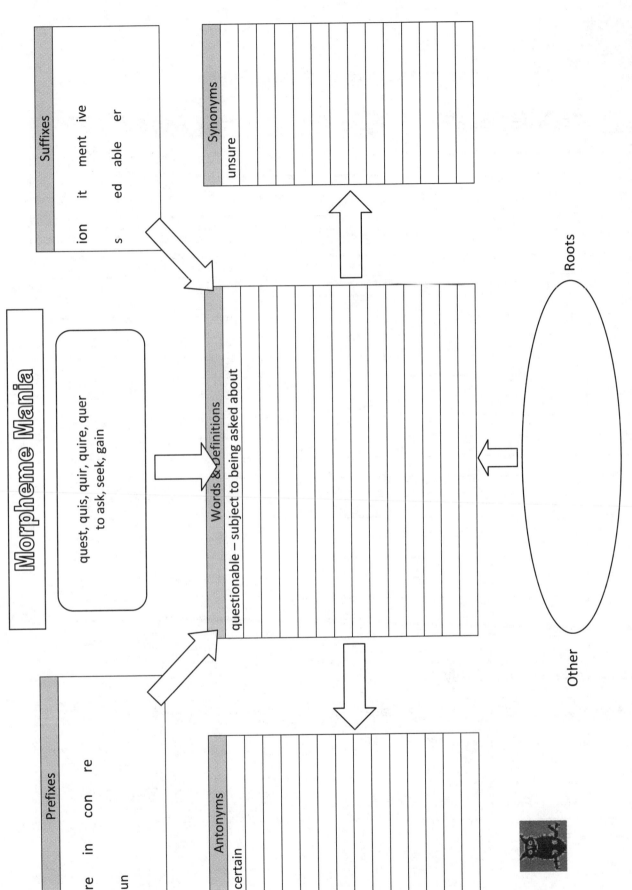

Root: *quest, quis, quir, quire, quer*

Word	Synonym / Antonym	Word	Synonym / Antonym

Morphemes for this meaning family

Prefixes	Roots	Suffixes

Root Squares

Name

How many words can you make?

Start in any square. Your goal is to combine two or more word parts to make as many words in the 'val, vali, vale, vail, valu, value' family as you can. Write each word and the definition you can think of for it in the space provided at the bottom of the page. Use the back of the page if you need to.

de	ent	e
ate	val, vali, vale, vail, valu, value	id
in	ion	equi

_____

_____

_____

_____

_____

_____

_____

_____

_____

_____

_____

Magic Squares

Name

Select the best answer for each of the words in the 'val, vali, vale, vail, valu, value' family from the numbered definitions. Put the number in the proper space in the Magic Square box. If the total of the numbers is the same both across and down, you have found the magic number!

'val, vali, vale, vail, valu, value' means strength, worth, health

WORDS	DEFINITIONS
A. equivalent	1. quality of being thoroughly strongest; quality of dominance
B. evaluating	2. having the same worth or strength
C. validated	3. lack of readiness to be of use or worth to
D. devalued	4. in a manner not having worth or strength
E. invalidly	5. strong or worthy for both; having opposing feelings or attitudes
F. valiant	6. took worth away from
G. valueless	7. declared that something has worth
H. ambivalent	8. possessing strength; brave and bold
I. unavailability	9. assessing the worth of; giving a grade to
	10. without worth

Magic Square Box

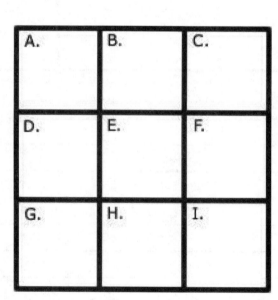

Magic Number ____

www.dynamicliteracy.com

Stair Steps

Name _____

Fill in the missing letters of each 'val, vali, vale, vail, valu, value' word by using the definitions
'val, vali, vale, vail, valu, value' means strength, worth, health

#											
1.	v	a	l								
2.	v	a	l	u	e						
3.	v	a	l								
4.			v	a	l						
5.			v	a	l	u					
6.	v	a	l								
7.		v	a	l	u						
8.				v	a	l					

1. strong and worthy; legitimate and creditable
2. worthwhile things; ethics, morals, or beliefs of emotional investments
3. in a manner having worth; in a way being legitimate
4. people lacking strength; people weak as a result of illness or injury
5. taking worth away from
6. declaring that something has worth
7. assessments of worth; acts of giving grades to
8. in a manner having the same worth or strength

A Bad Start but a Good Finish

Gore Mandizer, the famous food editor, wanted to <u>check out the worth</u> of the new restaurant in town. Because the restaurant advertised that a second dinner <u>of the same worth</u> as the first would be half price, Gore took along his friend Eppie Curean.

The restaurant's host and owner didn't recognize the critic and said there were no tables <u>ready to be of use or worth </u>to them, but Gore hinted strongly that if the owner <u>considered</u> his business <u>worthy</u>, he should find them a place to sit.

The owner got the hint and led and Gore and Eppie to a table and given menus that were stained with food. Gore and Eppie, <u>thinking that both to leave and to stay were strong choices</u>, decided to give it a try.

The rest of the experience was so good that Gore <u>in a strong manner</u> tried not to let them know who he was. The good food and service <u>took away the worth</u> of the original unpleasantry and they both though it a <u>worthwhile</u> experience. Gore and Eppie then had their parking permit <u>made worthy</u> and left.

Fill in the blanks below using words from the "val, vali, vale, vail, valu, value" family.

1. Gore and Eppie were _____ the new restaurant.

2. The prices of the two dinners were exactly _____.

3. Fortunately a table became _____ for Gore and Eppie.

4. The owner _____ his business and his customers.

5. The customers were _____ about whether to stay or leave.

6. The food critic _____ kept his identity hidden.

7. The quality of the rest of the evening _____ the original bad impressions.

8. Overall, the restaurant visit was a _____ experience.

9. The parking permit was _____ for customers.

Word Bank

ambivalent	equivalent	prevailed	valor
available	invalidated	valiantly	valuable
evaluating	invalidity	validated	valued

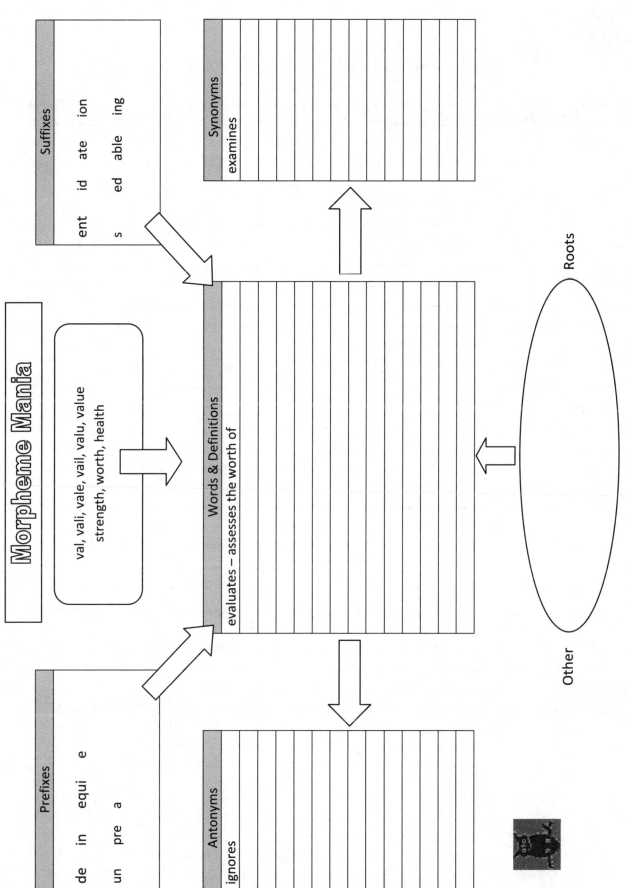

Morpheme Mania

Prefixes

de   in   equi   e

un   pre   a

Suffixes

ent   id   ate   ion

s   ed   able   ing

val, vali, vale, vail, valu, value
strength, worth, health

Words & Definitions

evaluates – assesses the worth of

Synonyms

examines

Antonyms

ignores

Roots

Other

Build as many words as you can for this root family. Use the prefixes and suffixes listed, or add your own. If you use any "combining roots", add them to the "Other Roots" box. Try to think of an antonym and a synonym for each word you build.

©2007 Dynamic Literacy, LLC

www.DynamicLiteracy.com

25

Name _____

Root: *val, vali, vale, vali, valu, value*

Word	Synonym / Antonym	Word	Synonym / Antonym

Morphemes for this meaning family

Prefixes	Roots	Suffixes

www.dynamicliteracy.com

Root Squares

How many words can you make?

Start in any square. Your goal is to combine two or more word parts to make as many words in the 'port' family as you can. Write each word and the definition you can think of for it in the space provided at the bottom of the page. Use the back of the page if you need to.

Name

er	trans	im
ed	port	re
sup	ing	ex

_____

_____

_____

_____

_____

_____

_____

_____

_____

_____

_____

Magic Squares

Name _____

Select the best answer for each of the words in the 'port' family from the numbered definitions. Put the number in the proper space in the Magic Square box. If the total of the numbers is the same both across and down, you have found the magic number!

'port' means to carry, bring

WORDS	DEFINITIONS
A. supportable	1. carried away from; expelled from a country
B. unsupported	2. people who bring back; people who give information about
C. reporters	3. in a manner carrying from beneath; in a manner that upholds or keeps from falling
D. transporters	4. people or vehicles that carry across
E. reporting	5. able to be brought in; able to be brought into the country to sell
F. exporters	6. people who carry out; people who send goods out of the country to sell
G. importable	7. not carried from beneath; not upheld or kept from falling
H. supportingly	8. bringing back; giving information about
I. transported	9. capable of being carried from beneath; able to be upheld or kept from falling
	10. carried across; brought from one place to another

Magic Square Box

A.	B.	C.
D.	E.	F.
G.	H.	I.

Magic Number ____

www.dynamicliteracy.com

Stair Steps

Name _____

Fill in the missing letters of each 'port' word by using the definitions below
'port' means to carry, bring

1. | | | p | o | r | t | | | | | | | |
2. | p | o | r | t | | | | | | | | |
3. | | | p | o | r | t | | | | | |
4. | | | p | o | r | t | | | | |
5. | | | p | o | r | t | | | |
6. | | | p | o | r | t | | |
7. | | | | | p | o | r | t | | |
8. | | | | | p | o | r | t | |
9. | | | | | p | o | r | t | | | | |

1. to carry out; to send goods out of the country to sell
2. people who carry
3. a person who brings back; a person who gives information about
4. carrying out; sending goods out of the country to sell
5. in a manner brought back; in a manner giving information about
6. in a manner worth being brought in; in a significant or relevant manner
7. people or vehicles that carry across
8. not capable of being carried from beneath; not able to be upheld or kept from falling
9. act or process of carrying across; a means of conveyance

www.dynamicliteracy.com

Off they Go!

Taiwo, Julian, and Irtefa were about to take their first airplane ride together. They were so excited. They especially liked the fact that a limousine would be <u>carrying them across</u> from their homes to the air terminal.

When they arrived at the terminal, they asked a <u>person who carries</u> to help them carry their luggage into the terminal. While they waited at the terminal, they watched trucks picking up the <u>goods sent in</u> from all over the world. They also saw cargo planes that were taking <u>goods to be sent out</u> to other places all over the world.

When they got onto the plane, Julian used his carry-on bag as a <u>carry under</u> for his feet, and Taiwo and Irtefa got out their <u>able to be carried</u> headrests and settled into their seats. The attendant <u>brought back</u> information that they would depart in ten minutes but that it was very <u>relevant</u> that they buckle up in their seatbelts now. Soon, the feel of the plane rushing into the sky felt great to the three friends and off they went.

Fill in the blanks below using words from the "port" family.

1. The friends were excited that a limousine would be _____ them to the airport.

2. The airline _____ helped them carry all their luggage.

3. Trucks were picking up the _____ being delivered from other countries.

4. Cargo planes were taking _____ out to go to other countries.

5. Julian used a carry-on bag to _____ his feet.

6. The girls brought along convenient, _____ headrests for the long trip.

7. The flight attendant _____ that the plane would be leaving on time.

8. The friends were reminded that it is extremely _____ to buckle seatbelts.

Word Bank

deportment	exports	portable	support
deported	important	porter	supportingly
exportable	imports	reported	transporting

www.dynamicliteracy.com

Morpheme Mania

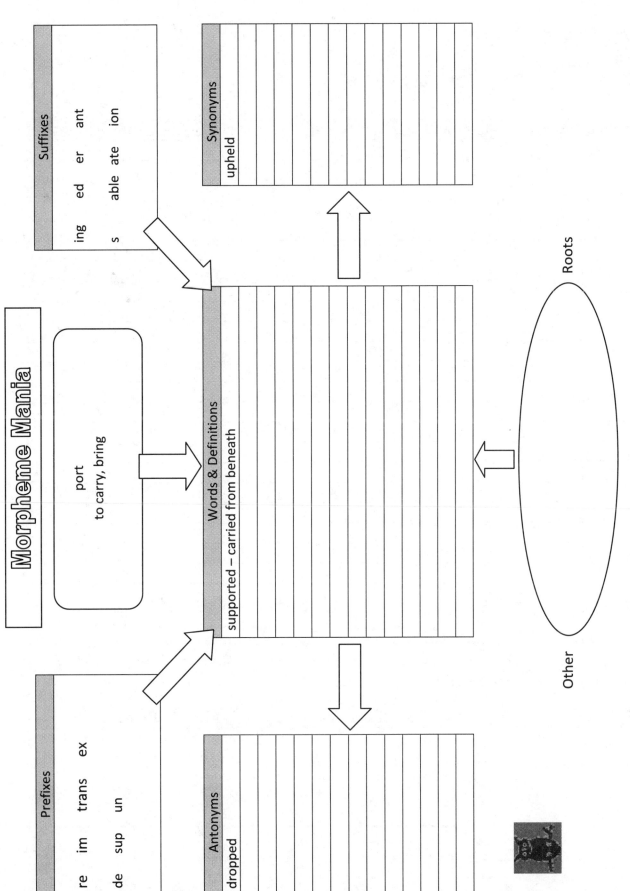

Prefixes

re   im   trans   ex

de   sup   un

Suffixes

ing   ed   er   ant

s   able   ate   ion

port
to carry, bring

Words & Definitions

supported – carried from beneath

Synonyms

upheld

Antonyms

dropped

Roots

Other

Build as many words as you can for this root family. Use the prefixes and suffixes listed, or add your own. If you use any "combining roots", add them to the "Other Roots" box. Try to think of an antonym and a synonym for each word you build.

31

My Word Wall

Root: *port*

Word	Synonym / Antonym	Word	Synonym / Antonym

Morphemes for this meaning family

Prefixes	Roots	Suffixes

www.dynamicliteracy.com

Root Squares

_____
Name

How many words can you make?

Start in any square. Your goal is to combine two or more word parts to make as many words in the 'ject' family as you can. Write each word and the definition you can think of for it in the space provided at the bottom of the page. Use the back of the page if you need to.

re	ion	ile
ory	ject	inter
sub	ure	pro

_____

_____

_____

_____

_____

_____

_____

_____

_____

_____

_____

Magic Squares

Name _____

Select the best answer for each of the words in the 'ject' family from the numbered definitions. Put the number in the proper space in the Magic Square box. If the total of the numbers is the same both across and down, you have found the magic number!

'ject' means to throw

WORDS	DEFINITIONS
A. adjective	1. something thrown in between; act of inserting or breaking into with a comment
B. reject	2. throwing out; driving out or expelling
C. projectile	3. throwing onto; a word that describes a noun
D. dejected	4. thrown down; disheartened or depressed
E. ejecting	5. something thrown forward; something shot forward
F. injections	6. related to throwing together; based on guesswork
G. objectionable	7. to throw back; to refuse or toss away
H. conjectural	8. able to be thrown up against; likely to be protested
I. interjection	9. acts of throwing into; acts of forcing or driving something in

Magic Square Box

A.	B.	C.
D.	E.	F.
G.	H.	I.

Magic Number ____

Stair Steps

Name

Fill in the missing letters of each 'ject' word by using the definitions below
'ject' means to throw

1. | | | j | e | c | t |
2. | | | j | e | c | t |
3. | | j | e | c | t |
4. | | j | e | c | t |
5. | | | j | e | c | t |
6. | | | j | e | c | t |
7. | | | | j | e | c | t |
8. | | j | e | c | t |

1. to throw back; to refuse or toss away
2. throws into; forces or drives something in
3. act of throwing out; an act of driving out or expelling
4. throwing onto; a word that describes a noun
5. something thrown forward; something shot forward
6. related to throwing together; based on guesswork
7. throwing between; inserting or breaking into with a comment
8. able to be thrown up against; likely to be protested

www.dynamicliteracy.com

Edward Jenner Takes a Bold Risk

Edward Jenner wanted to find a way to stop the disease cowpox. He had done lots of research but had found nothing. Feeling <u>thrown down</u>, he almost gave up. One day as he was tossing <u>things thrown across</u> the room at the wall, he had an idea. "Aha!" he said as he practically <u>threw</u> himself <u>out</u> of his seat. Jenner <u>threw together</u> ideas, thinking that <u>thrusting</u> a bit of the disease <u>into</u> someone could give immunity against that disease. His fellow townspeople were <u>throwing up obstacles in the way</u> against Jenner's idea and were <u>throwing</u> him <u>up</u> to harsh questions.   "Excuse me," one of the locals <u>threw in between</u> the arguments, "This is just too stupid and dangerous. "

But Jenner said he would <u>throw back</u> their fear and ridicule and would one day try out his theory. He did, successfully, and that is how vaccinations came to be.

Fill in the blanks below using words from the "ject" family.

1. Because he felt _____, Jenner almost gave up.

2. Jenner was one day wrapped in thought while hurling _____ across the room.

3. He was so excited that he _____ himself out of his chair.

4. He _____ in his thoughts that a bit of the disease could give immunity.

5. He would _____ a small amount of cowpox into a healthy person.

6. The local citizens _____ to this plan.

7. They _____ him to harsh questioning.

8. One citizen even _____ ridicule into the discussion.

9. Jenner _____ the critics and successfully stops the disease.

Word Bank

adjective	ejected	objected	subjected
conjectured	inject	objectionable	subjective
dejected	interjected	rejects	trajectories

Morpheme Mania

Prefixes

re pro inter ad

de sub in tra

Suffixes

ion ile ory

ive s ed

ject
to throw

Words & Definitions

dejection – state of being thrown down

Synonyms

depression

Antonyms

joy

Roots

Other

Build as many words as you can for this root family. Use the prefixes and suffixes listed, or add your own. If you use any "combining roots", add them to the "Other Roots" box. Try to think of an antonym and a synonym for each word you build.

Root: j*ect*

Word	Synonym / Antonym	Word	Synonym / Antonym

Morphemes for this meaning family

Prefixes	Roots	Suffixes

www.dynamicliteracy.com

Root Squares

Name

How many words can you make?

Start in any square. Your goal is to combine two or more word parts to make as many words in the 'sign, signi' family as you can. Write each word and the definition you can think of for it in the space provided at the bottom of the page. Use the back of the page if you need to.

fic	ment	de
ant	sign, signi	er
ate	as	al

Magic Squares

Select the best answer for each of the words in the 'sign, signi' family from the numbered definitions. Put the number in the proper space in the Magic Square box. If the total of the numbers is the same both across and down, you have found the magic number!

'sign, signi' means mark, seal; meaning; indication

WORDS	DEFINITIONS
A. assigning	1. to indicate completely; to hand over or deliver
B. designated	2. in a manner of no marked importance of things done; irrelevantly
C. insignificantly	3. marks of things done; importances
D. resignations	4. indications back; notifications of giving up a job or office
E. redesigning	5. a person's mark indicating who he or she is; a person's name as written by himself or herself
F. reassigned	6. gave a mark to again; gave a task again
G. signature	7. indicated; named or appointed
H. significances	8. marking down again; sketching out a new or different plan
I. reassign	9. giving a mark to; giving a task
	10. to give a mark to again; to give a task again

Magic Square Box

A.	B.	C.
D.	E.	F.
G.	H.	I.

Magic Number ____

Stair Steps

Name _____

Fill in the missing letters of each 'sign, signi' word by using the definitions below
'sign, signi' means mark, seal; meaning; indication

1. | s | i | g | n | | |

2. | | | s | i | g | n | |

3. | | | s | i | g | n | | |

4. | s | i | g | n | | | | |

5. | s | i | g | n | | | | | |

6. | | | s | i | g | n | | | | |

7. | | | s | i | g | n | | | | | |

8. | | | | s | i | g | n | | | | | |

9. | | | s | i | g | n | i | | | | | | |

1. a person who indicates; a person communicating by hand language
2. gives a mark to; gives a task
3. a person who marks down; a person who sketches out a plan
4. people who indicate; people who give non-verbal messages
5. people's marks indicating who they are; people's names as written by themselves
6. acts or processes of giving a mark to; tasks
7. an acts or processes of indicating; names or appointments
8. acts or processes of giving a mark to again; tasks given again
9. quality of making no marked importance; irrelevance

   www.dynamicliteracy.com

A Historical Connection

The detail most <u>marked with importance</u> about Morgan's family history was the fact that a distant relative had been one of the original <u>markers of his name</u> of the Declaration of Independence. When Morgan's teacher <u>marked off as a task</u> to the class to do a family history project, Morgan pleaded with his parents to make a trip to Washington, D.C., to view the document in person. They agreed that it would be a creative addition to the <u>marked task given him</u>.

After turning at the printed street <u>indications</u>, and traffic <u>markers</u>, the family arrived in front of the National Archives. This building is <u>marked down in purpose</u> as housing a collection of all the major papers of America's government.   Lines of history buffs waiting to see the Declaration snaked around the building, but Morgan kept busy checking out the intricate <u>sketches marked down</u> all around the building's walls. Finally, the group with Morgan's family filed past the display case that contained the Declaration of Independence, and Morgan smiled as he read the <u>name markers</u> at the bottom of the document.

Picking up a brochure as he was leaving the building, Morgan said to his mother, "I'm **so** going to get an A."

Fill in the blanks below using words from the "sign, signi" family.

1. Morgan's ancestor was a _____ contributor to American history.

2. That ancestor was a _____ of the Declaration of Independence.

3. When the teacher _____ the project, Morgan realized he could use the Declaration of Independence as a research source.

4. The _____ that Morgan received from his teacher was to connect his family and history in some way.

5. Street and traffic _____ led the family to the right place.

6. The National Archives is _____ as a repository for America's historical papers.

7. Examining the _____ on the building's walls helped Morgan pass the time in line.

8. The clear _____ at the bottom of the Declaration was easy for Morgan to read.

Word Bank

assigned	designee	resign	signer
assignment	designs	signature	significant
designated	redesign	signals	signature

www.dynamicliteracy.com

Morpheme Mania

Prefixes

de   as   con   re

in

Suffixes

fic   ant   er   ment

ate   s   al   ing   er

sign, signi

mark, seal; meaning; indication

Words & Definitions

consign – to indicate completely or hand over

Synonyms

assign

Antonyms

retain

Roots

Other

Build as many words as you can for this root family. Use the prefixes and suffixes listed, or add your own. If you use any "combining roots", add them to the "Other Roots" box. Try to think of an antonym and a synonym for each word you build.

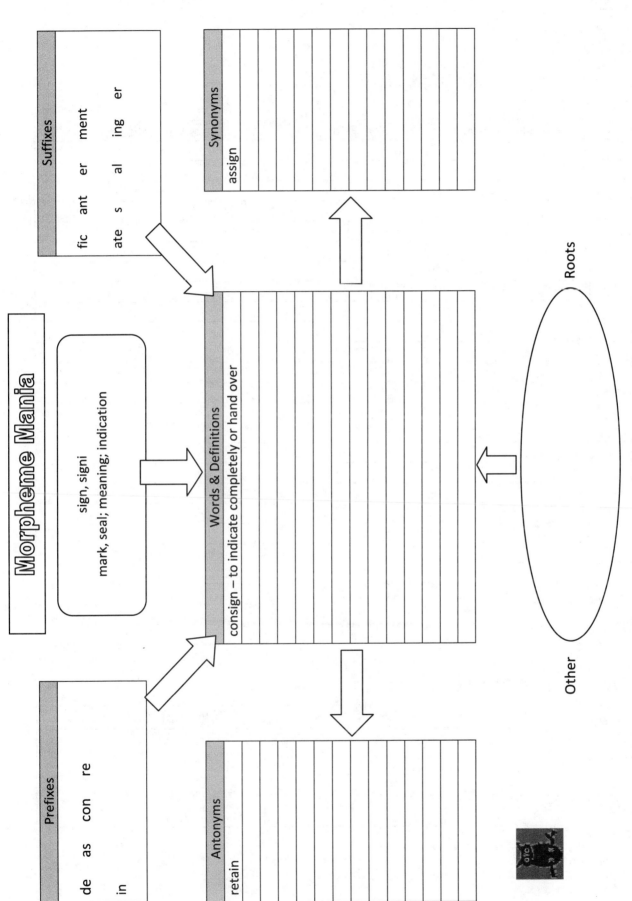

Root: *sign, signi*

Word	Synonym / Antonym	Word	Synonym / Antonym

Morphemes for this meaning family

Prefixes	Roots	Suffixes

www.dynamicliteracy.com

Root Squares

How many words can you make?

Start in any square. Your goal is to combine two or more word parts to make as many words in the 'st, sta, stas, stat, state' family as you can. Write each word and the definition you can think of for it in the space provided at the bottom of the page. Use the back of the page if you need to.

ion	circum	contra
ance	st, sta, stas, stat, state	ment
di	ant	ly

Magic Squares

Select the best answer for each of the words in the 'st, sta, stas, stat, state' family from the numbered definitions. Put the number in the proper space in the Magic Square box. If the total of the numbers is the same both across and down, you have found the magic number!

'st, sta, stas, stat, state' means to stand, stop

WORDS

A. circumstances
B. contrasted
C. statement
D. stance
E. stably
F. equidistantly
G. distantly
H. stations
I. thermostat

DEFINITIONS

1. time at which the sun seems to stand still
2. stood one thing with another; compared one thing to another
3. device to make temperature stand at a fixed point
4. a specific stand; a person's point in view
5. in a manner standing apart; far
6. in a manner able to stand; in a firm or unchanging manner
7. a stand; a specific declaration
8. so as to stand at a balanced space away from
9. things standing around; situations having a bearing on an event
10. stands, as for trains, buses, and taxis

Magic Square Box

A.	B.	C.
D.	E.	F.
G.	H.	I.

Magic Number ____

www.dynamicliteracy.com

Stair Steps

Name

Fill in the missing letters of each 'st, sta, stas, stat, state' word by using the definitions below
'st, sta, stas, stat, state' means to stand, stop

1. | s | t | a | t | | |
2. | | | s | t | |
3. | | | s | t | | |
4. | | | | | | s | t |
5. | | | s | t | | | |
6. | | | | | | s | t |
7. | | | | | | s | t |
8. | | | | | | s | t | | | |

1. took a stand; declared
2. standing in; immediate
3. the space between things standing apart
4. stands one thing with another; compares one thing to another
5. causing to stand apart; spacing apart
6. standing one thing with another; comparing one thing to another
7. a thing standing around; a situation having a bearing on an event
8. qualities of standing at a balanced space away from

www.dynamicliteracy.com

Custer's Last Stand

The Battle of the Little Bighorn, also known as Custer's Last Stand, took place on June 25-26, 1876 near the Little Bighorn River in Eastern Montana. The <u>things standing around</u> that led to this battle between the U.S. Cavalry and the Lakota and Northern Cheyenne Indians (Native Americans) were related to the fact that many Indians <u>stood apart</u> from their reservations. Their <u>specific stand</u> was that they should be free to live wherever they wanted. General Custer and other cavalry commanders sought to make the Indians home <u>unchanging or standing thoroughly</u>.

General Custer thought that if he could capture all of the Native Americans who had left the reservations and return them there, he could achieve a <u>quality of being able to stand firm</u> for the area. General Custer's own <u>stands, or specific declarations</u>, show that he thought the battle would be easy. However, when Custer's <u>idea is stood with what actually took place</u>, it is clear that he miscalculated the strength and resolve of the Native Americans.

The usual way the Cavalry fought, <u>standing at a balanced space away from</u> each other, didn't work, because there were so many Indians that the line of troops became <u>not able to stand firm</u>. Once this happened, <u>the space standing between</u> the Cavalrymen became too large and the battle was lost.

Fill in the blanks below using words from the "st, sta, stas, stat, state" family.

1. Many _____ led to the Indian Wars and the Battle of the Little Bighorn.

2. Thousands of Native Americans _____ themselves from their reservations.

3. Many took the position, or _____ that they should be able to move freely about.

4. A _____ place to live means standing in one place.

5. _____ the quality of standing firm, is something every government seeks.

6. Custer's _____ show that he underestimated his opponent.

7. Often, when ideas are compared or _____ new understandings emerge.

8. If three cavalrymen are standing _____ to one another, they are all the same length apart.

9. Once the battle lines became _____ Custer's strategy began to fail.

10. As soon as the _____ between men became great enough, the battle was over.

Word Bank

distanced	distance	ecstatic	stability
circumstances	constant	stance	statements
contrasted	distantly	unstable	equidistant

www.dynamicliteracy.com

Morpheme Mania

Prefixes

circum di equi con

contra in

Suffixes

ion ance ment ant

ly s abil ize

st, sta, stas, stat, state
to stand, stop

Words & Definitions

stable – able to stand firm

Synonyms

sturdy

Antonyms

wobbly

Roots

Other

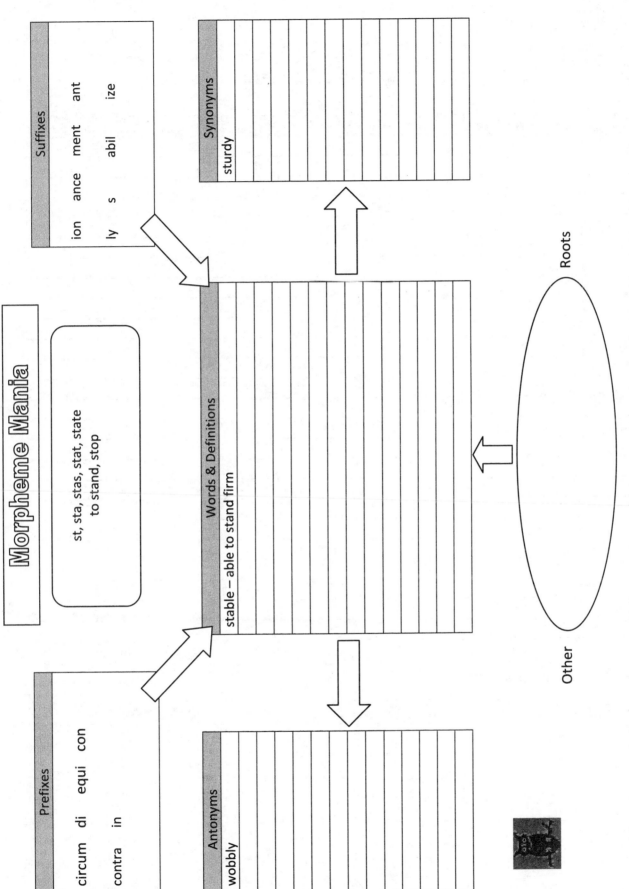

Build as many words as you can for this root family. Use the prefixes and suffixes listed, or add your own. If you use any "combining roots", add them to the "Other Roots" box. Try to think of an antonym and a synonym for each word you build.

Root: *st, sta, stas, stat, state*

Word	Synonym / Antonym	Word	Synonym / Antonym

Morphemes for this meaning family

Prefixes	Roots	Suffixes

www.dynamicliteracy.com

Root Squares

Name

How many words can you make?

Start in any square. Your goal is to combine two or more word parts to make as many words in the 'act, ag' family as you can. Write each word and the definition you can think of for it in the space provided at the bottom of the page. Use the back of the page if you need to.

ive	or	ate
re	act, ag	inter
en	ent	in

_____

_____

_____

_____

_____

_____

_____

_____

_____

_____

_____

_____

_____

Magic Squares

Select the best answer for each of the words in the 'act, ag' family from the numbered definitions. Put the number in the proper space in the Magic Square box. If the total of the numbers is the same both across and down, you have found the magic number!

'act, ag' means to do; to perform; to cause to move

WORDS	DEFINITIONS
A. activate	1. causing rays to move spontaneously; emitting nuclear particles
B. interactive	2. to set in motion
C. reactions	3. having excessive motion; overdoing
D. enacting	4. the state of not doing anything
E. inactivity	5. caused substances to move into one mass
F. agents	6. putting into motion; making into law
G. reactors	7. performances or movements in response to something
H. coagulated	8. forces that cause change or movement
I. hyperactive	9. serving to do or move between each other
	10. people or things that perform or move in response; machines causing nuclei to respond stimuli

Magic Square Box

A.	B.	C.
D.	E.	F.
G.	H.	I.

Magic Number ____

www.dynamicliteracy.com

Stair Steps

Name

Fill in the missing letters of each 'act, ag' word by using the definitions below
'act, ag' means to do; to perform; to cause to move

1. | a | g | | | |

2. | a | c | t | | |

3. | | | a | c | t | |

4. | | | a | c | t | |

5. | | | a | g | |

6. | a | c | t | |

7. | a | c | t | |

8. | | | | | a | c | t |

1. a force that causes change or movement
2. people who perform or do; stage or film performers
3. put into motion; made into law
4. lack of performance or movement
5. to cause substances to move into one mass
6. movements; states of being in motion
7. processes or ways of setting things in motion
8. processes of doing or moving between each other

www.dynamicliteracy.com

Class Play

The favorite <u>performance</u> of the students of Happydays School was always the end-of-the-year play. This year was special because the parents of the students in upper grades would be present. Zach was elected director, and his ideas for the play quickly began to <u>move together as a mass</u> in his brain. The big challenge, he thought, was getting as many students, in his homeroom as well as the other homerooms, to be <u>people to perform on stage</u>. He decided that instead of presenting one play, the class would do many short skits instead. Zach's principal <u>moved</u> favorably <u>in response</u> to the idea.

Zach put many of his classmates in charge of the skits that were historical events put on as <u>processes of causing to be done again</u>. The variety of skits and the number of roles that were required allowed students throughout the school to <u>perform among themselves</u>. No one was <u>not doing</u> anything during the rehearsals because there was so much to do.

On the night of the performance, Zach hopped around, <u>having excessive motion</u>. He was exhausted, but happy as he listened to applause from classmates and their parents.

Fill in the blanks below using words from the "act, ag" family.

1. The end-of-year play is a busy final _____ at Happydays School.

2. The many ideas that Zach had for the play finally began to _____ into a single thought.

3. Students in other classes were recruited to be _____ in the skits.

4. The principal must have liked Zach's idea because she _____ to it well.

5. Zach's class play was a series of skits that were _____ of historic events.

6. Students from all the classes _____ with each other during the skits.

7. With so much to do, there was not an _____ student at any rehearsal.

8. Because of all his scurrying around during the performance, audience members might have thought he was _____.

Word Bank

activity	coagulate	inactive	interaction
actors	enact	inaction	reacted
agilely	hyperactive	interacted	reenactments

www.dynamicliteracy.com

Morpheme Mania

Prefixes

inter   re   en   in

co

Suffixes

ive   ate   or   ent

ity   s   ion   or   ist

act, ag
to do; to perform; to cause to move

Words & Definitions

activist – a person who favors direct movement

Synonyms

advocate

Antonyms

bystander

Roots

radio

Other

Build as many words as you can for this root family. Use the prefixes and suffixes listed, or add your own. If you use any "combining roots", add them to the "Other Roots" box. Try to think of an antonym and a synonym for each word you build.

My Word Wall

Name _____

Root: *act, ag*

Word	Synonym / Antonym	Word	Synonym / Antonym

Morphemes for this meaning family

Prefixes	Roots	Suffixes

Copyright Dynamic Literacy, LLC   www.dynamicliteracy.com

Root Squares

How many words can you make?

Start in any square. Your goal is to combine two or more word parts to make as many words in the 'pel, pul, pell, puls, pulse' family as you can. Write each word and the definition you can think of for it in the space provided at the bottom of the page. Use the back of the page if you need to.

com	ive	dis
ion	pel, pul, pell, puls, pulse	pro
ex	ent	re

_____

_____

_____

_____

_____

_____

_____

_____

_____

_____

_____

_____

Magic Squares

Name _____

Select the best answer for each of the words in the 'pel, pul, pell, puls, pulse' family from the numbered definitions. Put the number in the proper space in the Magic Square box. If the total of the numbers is the same both across and down, you have found the magic number!

'pel, pul, pell, puls, pulse' means to push, force, beat

WORDS	DEFINITIONS
A. compellent	1. pushed or forced into
B. propellers	2. instruments that push forward
C. expulsion	3. pushed or forced out
D. repellents	4. substances that serve to push back; substances that act to drive back or keep away
E. dispelled	5. pushed or beat; throbbed
F. impulsive	6. pushed away; drove out
G. pulsated	7. the act or process of pushing or forcing out
H. repulsive	8. likely to drive or push into
I. expelled	9. tending to push together; tending to force
	10. likely to push back; offensive

Magic Square Box

A.	B.	C.
D.	E.	F.
G.	H.	I.

Magic Number ____

www.dynamicliteracy.com

Stair Steps

Name

Fill in the missing letters of each 'pel, pul, pell, puls, pulse' word by using the definitions below
'pel, pul, pell, puls, pulse' means to push, force, beat

1.			p	e	l						
2.			p	e	l						
3.	p	u	l	s							
4.			p	e	l	l					
5.			p	e	l	l					
6.				p	e	l	l				
7.				p	u	l	s				

1. to push or force into
2. pushes back; drives back or keeps away
3. pushing or beating; throbbing
4. a person or tool that pushes or forces into
5. serving or tending to push back; acting to drive back or tending to keep away
6. pushing away; driving out
7. acts or processes of pushing forward

www.dynamicliteracy.com

...3,2,1, Blastoff!

Astronauts have different reasons that <u>push or force</u> them to train for a space expedition. Some may desire fame, some adventure, but many just have a <u>forceful push</u> to travel fast. Much training, though, is required before an astronaut is ready to be <u>pushed forward</u> into space.

Early flight training often comes at the stick of an airplane powered by <u>instruments that push</u> forward instead of by more advanced rockets.   Math classes examining <u>the process of pushing forward</u> in jets are also required. People who want to become astronauts must master a flight simulator that mimics the weightless conditions that they will find in space.

All this training leads to the big moment when the clock <u>beats or pushes</u> down the seconds...3,2,1, and the spaceship is <u>pushed out</u> from Earth's atmosphere. The firing of the engines sends <u>acts of pushing or throbbing</u> of light through the small windows of the space capsule. A modern explorer to rival Christopher Columbus is launched.

Fill in the blanks below using words from the "pel, pul, pell, puls, pulse" family.

1. There are many reasons that _____ astronauts to enter the space program.

2. Like other explorers, astronauts can have a _____ to seek fame or speed.

3. Before he or she can be _____ into space, an astronaut must be trained.

4. Airplanes that move forward with _____ are less technically advanced than rockets.

5. The study of _____ , forward motion, includes advanced mathematics.

6. The second-by-second _____ of the clock count the time down to the launch of the space ship.

7. A spaceship is _____ from Earth's atmosphere when it is launched.

8. _____ of light came through the windows from the engine firings.

Word Bank

compel	impelling	propulsion	repel
compulsion	propelled	pulsations	repellent
expelled	propellers	pulses	repulsive

Morpheme Mania

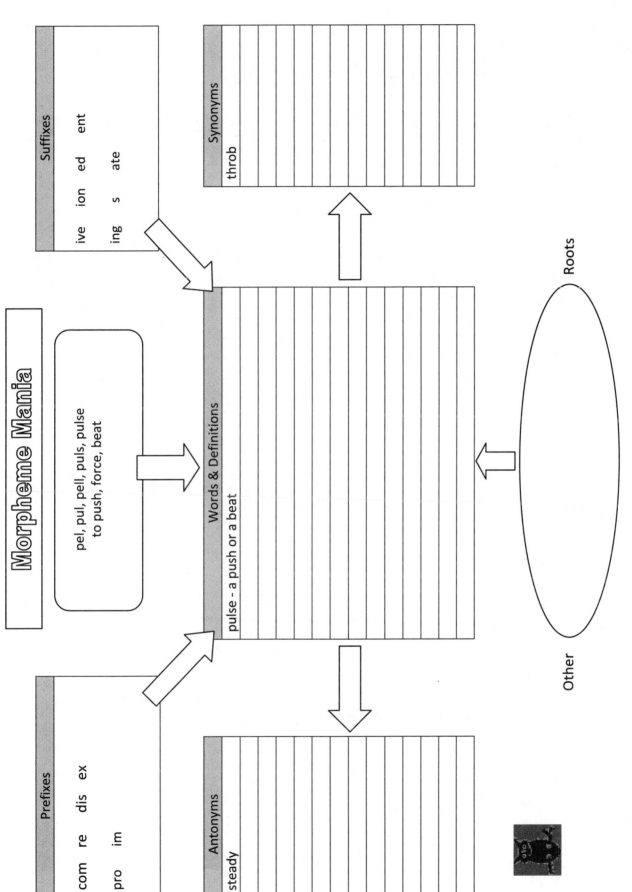

Prefixes

com   re   dis   ex

pro   im

Suffixes

ive   ion   ed   ent

ing   s   ate

pel, pul, pell, puls, pulse
to push, force, beat

Words & Definitions

pulse – a push or a beat

Synonyms

throb

Antonyms

steady

Roots

Other

Build as many words as you can for this root family. Use the prefixes and suffixes listed, or add your own. If you use any "combining roots", add them to the "Other Roots" box. Try to think of an antonym and a synonym for each word you build.

©2007 Dynamic Literacy, LLC

www.DynamicLiteracy.com

My Word Wall

Name

Root: *pel, pul, pell, puls, pulse*

Word	Synonym / Antonym	Word	Synonym / Antonym

Morphemes for this meaning family

Prefixes	Roots	Suffixes

Root Squares

How many words can you make?

Start in any square. Your goal is to combine two or more word parts to make as many words in the 'jur, jure, juri, jury, juris, jus, just' family as you can. Write each word and the definition you can think of for it in the space provided at the bottom of the page. Use the back of the page if you need to.

ment	ad	ed
ice	jur, jure, juri, jury, juris, jus, just	in
re	or	able

_____
_____
_____
_____
_____
_____
_____
_____
_____
_____
_____
_____
_____
_____

Magic Squares

Name

Select the best answer for each of the words in the 'jur, jure, juri, jury, juris, jus, just' family from the numbered definitions. Put the number in the proper space in the Magic Square box. If the total of the numbers is the same both across and down, you have found the magic number!

'jur, jure, juri, jury, juris, jus, just' means law; right, true; to swear an oath

WORDS

A. adjusted
B. unjustly
C. adjustment
D. injuries
E. readjustable
F. conjurors
G. reinjured
H. perjuring
I. injustices

DEFINITIONS

1. area of authority to state and enforce the law
2. act of changing toward what is right; correction
3. making a thoroughly false oath
4. deeds not right or lawful; harmful things
5. did something not right or lawful; harmed again
6. people who swear oaths together; people who call up a magic spirit
7. in a manner not correct according to law
8. able to be changed again toward what is right
9. changed toward what is right; corrected
10. situations that are not right or lawful; acts of unfairness

Magic Square Box

A.	B.	C.
D.	E.	F.
G.	H.	I.

Magic Number _____

www.dynamicliteracy.com

Stair Steps

Fill in the missing letters of each 'jur, jure, juri, jury, juris, jus, just' word by using the definitions
'jur, jure, juri, jury, juris, jus, just' means law; right, true; to swear an oath

1. | j | u | r | | |
2. | j | u | s | t | |
3. | | | | j | u | r | e |
4. | | | j | u | r |
5. | | | j | u | s | t |
6. | | | j | u | s | t |
7. | | | j | u | s | t |
8. | | | | j | u | s | t |
9. | | | j | u | s | t |

1. a person who serves to consider what is right; a panelist
2. in a manner correct according to law
3. to make a thoroughly false oath
4. people who do things not right or lawful; people who harm
5. changing toward what is right; correcting
6. situations that are not right or lawful; acts of unfairness
7. acts of changing toward what is right; corrections
8. act of changing again toward what is right
9. not able to be argued right and lawful; not defensible

Mock Trial

For their project on <u>fairness</u>, the class decided to hold a mock trial of the Pied Piper of Hamelin. Officers of the court, lawyers for both sides, the Pied Piper, and <u>panel that serves to decide what is right</u> were chosen from the class.

Plaintiffs in the case were the townspeople of Hamelin who thought that the Piper's demand of payment was <u>not able to be argued as right and lawful</u>. They also argued that acts hurting the children as punishment for the town's non-payment were great <u>harmful deeds that are not right</u> to them. The deal with the Piper had to <u>be changed toward what is right</u>. The Piper, they argued, should have to restore the children to the town.

Defending himself, the Piper held that he had been treated <u>in a manner not correct in law</u> by the town's officials when they withheld payment for ridding the town of its rats. He further <u>argued to be right and lawful</u> his position by producing a contract signed by the city's mayor. Then each <u>person who considers what is right</u> retired to think about the case.

Who suffered the worse <u>harmful deed</u>: the Piper for non-payment, or the town for the kidnapping of the children? What would you decide?

<u>Fill in the blanks below using words from the "jur, jure, juri, jury, juris, jus, just" family</u>.

1.   Everyone deserves _____ and equal treatment.

2.   The group that finally decides guilt or innocence is the _____.

3.   Excessive demands and false arguments are _____ in a court case.

4.   The townspeople suffered many _____ by losing their children.

5.   The people felt that the contract needed to be _____ and altered.

6.   The Piper felt that he had been _____ treated by the people.

7.   The Piper _____ his actions since he had not been paid.

8.   Each _____ of the panel had to decide what was right.

9.   Which side suffered the greater _____?

<u>Word Bank</u>

adjusted	injustice	justice	reinjures
adjusting	juror	justified	unjustifiable
injuries	jury	perjury	unjustly

www.dynamicliteracy.com

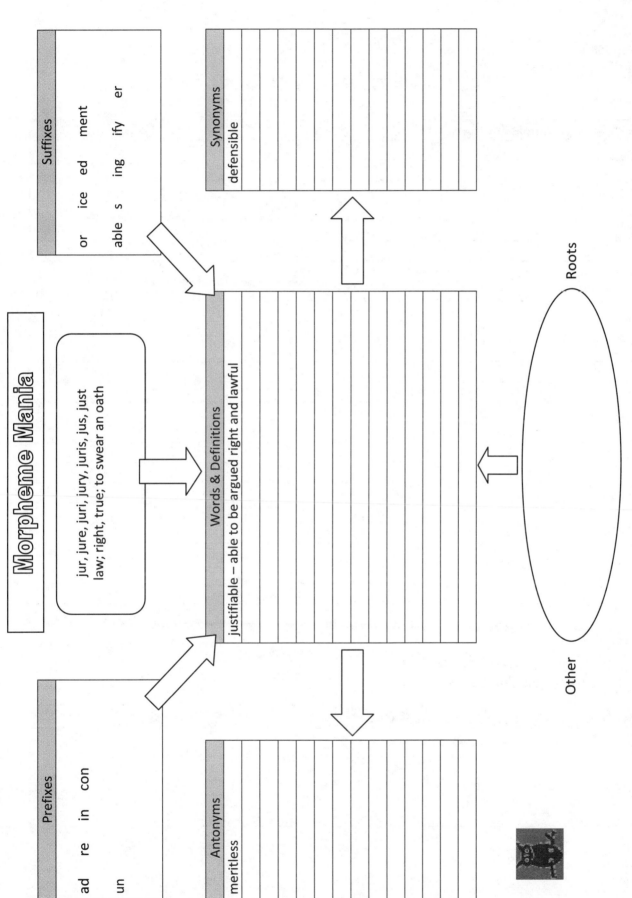

Morpheme Mania

Prefixes

ad   re   in   con

un

jur, jure, juri, jury, juris, jus, just

law; right, true; to swear an oath

Suffixes

or   ice   ed   ment

able   s   ing   ify   er

Words & Definitions

justifiable – able to be argued right and lawful

Synonyms

defensible

Antonyms

meritless

Other   Roots

Build as many words as you can for this root family. Use the prefixes and suffixes listed, or add your own. If you use any "combining roots", add them to the "Other Roots" box. Try to think of an antonym and a synonym for each word you build.

My Word Wall

Root: *jur, jure, juri, jury, juris, jus, just*

Word	Synonym / Antonym	Word	Synonym / Antonym

Morphemes for this meaning family

Prefixes	Roots	Suffixes

www.dynamicliteracy.com

Root Squares

How many words can you make?

Start in any square. Your goal is to combine two or more word parts to make as many words in the 'grad, grade, gress' family as you can. Write each word and the definition you can think of for it in the space provided at the bottom of the page. Use the back of the page if you need to.

trans	ive	ag
pro	grad, grade, gress	ion
di	uate	con

_____

_____

_____

_____

_____

_____

_____

_____

_____

_____

_____

_____

www.dynamicliteracy.com

Magic Squares

Name

Select the best answer for each of the words in the 'grad, grade, gress' family from the numbered definitions. Put the number in the proper space in the Magic Square box. If the total of the numbers is the same both across and down, you have found the magic number!

'grad, grade, gress' means step; to go

WORDS	DEFINITIONS
A. aggressions	1. stepping down; demeaning
B. transgressor	2. an act or process of going forward
C. progression	3. completing necessary steps; measuring in steps
D. digressed	4. went off apart; wandered or rambled
E. congressional	5. a measurement with 100 steps or degrees
F. regressed	6. stepped back; became worse
G. centigrade	7. a person who steps across or beyond; a person who does wrong
H. graduating	8. pertaining to a group that walks or goes together; relating to a council
I. gradual	9. acts of stepping toward; hostilities
	10. in steps; by slow movements

Magic Square Box

A.	B.	C.
D.	E.	F.
G.	H.	I.

Magic Number ____

www.dynamicliteracy.com

Stair Steps

Fill in the missing letters of each 'grad, grade, gress' word by using the definitions below
'grad, grade, gress' means step; to go

1. | g | r | a | d | | |

2. | | | g | r | e | s | s |

3. | | | | g | r | e | s | s |

4. | | | g | r | e | s | s |

5. | | | | g | r | e | s | s |

6. | | | g | r | e | s | s |

7. | | | g | r | e | s | s |

8. | | | g | r | e | s | s |

9. | | | | | g | r | e | s | s |

1. evaluated according to steps; assessed according to stages in a sequence
2. to go off apart; to wander or ramble
3. a group that walks or goes together; a council
4. anything that steps toward; a hostile person
5. went forward; advanced
6. acts of going apart; acts of wandering or rambling
7. in a manner stepping toward; in a hostile manner
8. in a manner moving forward in steps
9. acts of stepping across or beyond; violations

www.dynamicliteracy.com

 Useless, Never-ending Work

King Sisyphus, who thought he was better and smarter than the gods of Greece, once managed to tie up Hades, the god of the underworld, so that nothing on earth would die. This <u>step across in violation</u> against gods and men halted the natural <u>stepping forward</u> of life and death. Even warriors, hacked to bits in battle, would not die, and <u>in slow-step manner</u> the earth became too crowded. Hades finally escaped from Sisyphus' trickery and ordered him to appear in the underworld for punishment.

However, Sisyphus had another trick up his sleeve. Planning in <u>step together</u> with his wife, Sisyphus arranged not to have an official funeral service. When he got to the underworld, he <u>stepped back</u> to childish behavior and begged Queen Persephone to allow him to go home for a proper burial. (Queen Persephone is in the underworld herself as a result of a trick, but we must not <u>step apart</u> from Sisyphus' story.)

Hades grows angry <u>in a manner moving forward</u> with Sisyphus and sentences him to eternal labor. Sisyphus' task is to roll a boulder up a steep hill, a task that he undertakes <u>in a hostile manner</u>, sweat popping from his brow. After he rolls the boulder to the top of the hill, it rolls back down the steep <u>slope</u>. Sisyphus has to start all over again and again forever.

Fill in the blanks below using words from the "grad, grade, gress" family.

1. Sisyphus made some serious _____ against the rules of gods and men.

2. There is a natural _____ in life as we are born, grow up, and pass from earth.

3. _____, earth filled up with too many people.

4. Sisyphus' wife planned in _____ with him as to how to trick Hades' again.

5. In order to sweet-talk the queen, Sisyphus _____ to the habits of a young child.

6. Telling Persephone's story would be to _____ from the story of Sisyphus.

7. Hades' ill will toward Sisyphus piled up as he became _____ angrier.

8. Sisyphus pushes the bolder so _____ that it becomes a tough workout.

9. The steep _____ of the hill made Sisyphus' task even harder.

Word Bank

aggressively	degrading	grader	progressively
centigrade	digress	gradually	regressed
congress	grade	progression	transgression

www.dynamicliteracy.com

Morpheme Mania

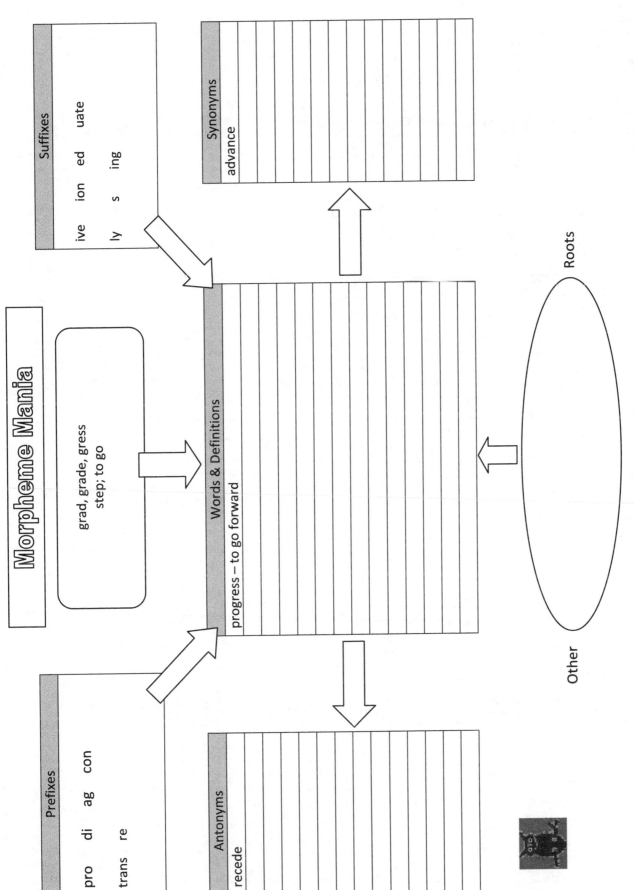

Prefixes

pro di ag con

trans re

grad, grade, gress
step; to go

Suffixes

ive ion ed uate

ly s ing

Words & Definitions

progress – to go forward

Synonyms

advance

Antonyms

recede

Roots

Other

Build as many words as you can for this root family. Use the prefixes and suffixes listed, or add your own. If you use any "combining roots", add them to the "Other Roots" box. Try to think of an antonym and a synonym for each word you build.

My Word Wall

Root: *grad, grade, gress*

Word	Synonym / Antonym	Word	Synonym / Antonym

Morphemes for this meaning family

Prefixes	Roots	Suffixes

www.dynamicliteracy.com

Root Squares

How many words can you make?

Start in any square. Your goal is to combine two or more word parts to make as many words in the 'graph' family as you can. Write each word and the definition you can think of for it in the space provided at the bottom of the page. Use the back of the page if you need to.

para	ic	auto
er	graph	poly
bio	tele	y

_____

_____

_____

_____

_____

_____

_____

_____

_____

_____

_____

Magic Squares

Name _____

Select the best answer for each of the words in the 'graph' family from the numbered definitions. Put the number in the proper space in the Magic Square box. If the total of the numbers is the same both across and down, you have found the magic number!

'graph' means something written, drawn, or recorded; chart

WORDS

A. autobiographic
B. biography
C. paragraphs
D. telegraphic
E. polygraph
F. geography
G. photographer
H. geographic
I. graphite

DEFINITIONS

1. the drawing of a region; the layout of the land
2. indicating marks beside groups of written ideas; collections of sentences which conc[e] notion
3. related to writing about the earth
4. relating to a written message sent over a distance
5. a person who records images on light-sensitive paper; a person who takes pictures
6. the drawing of the features of the earth
7. a writing about a person's life
8. a device that records many bits of data; a lie-detector
9. of a person's life story written by that person
10. substance used for writing; pencil lead

Magic Square Box

A.	B.	C.
D.	E.	F.
G.	H.	I.

Magic Number _____

www.dynamicliteracy.com

Stair Steps

Fill in the missing letters of each 'graph' word by using the definitions below
'graph' means something written, drawn, or recorded; chart

1. | g | r | a | p | h | | |

2. | g | r | a | p | h | |

3. | | | | g | r | a | p | h |

4. | | | | g | r | a | p | h |

5. | | | g | r | a | p | h |

6. | | | g | r | a | p | h |

7. | | | | g | r | a | p | h |

8. | | | g | r | a | p | h | | | | |

1. recorded; charted
2. detailed recordings; explicit representations
3. an indicating mark beside a written idea; a collection of sentences concerning a notion
4. devices that record many bits of data; lie-detectors
5. writings about people's lives
6. sending a written message over a distance
7. people who record images on light-sensitive paper; people who take pictures
8. in a manner related to the writing about a life

www.dynamicliteracy.com

It's About Writing

Ever since cavemen made <u>detailed recordings</u> on their walls to illustrate their lives, humans have been interested in the lives and endeavors of others. Many people agree that <u>writings about a person's life</u> and <u>writings about a person's life written by that very person</u> are the most interesting non-fiction to read. Where else can a reader find the juicy details of the <u>multi-charted lie-detector</u> results of a famous criminal, the inspirations behind the <u>light-image recordings</u> of Ansel Adams, or the life story of the inventor of the <u>device to send messages over a distance</u>?

In fact, one way to get to know yourself well is to write a story <u>relating to your life written by yourself</u>. Begin by <u>recording in chart form</u> the events of your life that have had an impact on your personality, including either photographs or your own drawings. Next, focus on a few of the most important and be <u>detailed in recording</u>. It doesn't matter whether you use keyboard or a pencil with <u>lead</u> to tell your story. Once you're famous you'll be glad you've already started to share your life with the world.

<u>Fill in the blanks below using words from the "graph" family</u>.

1. Cave paintings are considered the earliest _____ created by human beings.

2. _____ are life stories written by someone other than themselves.

3. Writings by people about their very own life stories are called _____.

4. Criminals fear _____ because they expose their many lies.

5. Ansel Adams' talent was taking black and white _____ of scenes in nature.

6. The _____ conveys writing to places some distance from each other.

7. Most of the works by Dickens, reflecting his own life, are _____ in nature.

8. _____ an outline of what they want to tell helps writers organize their big ideas.

9. A _____ description lets a reader actually see and feel a written event.

10. Writing pencils contain a carbon mineral called _____.

<u>Word Bank</u>

autobiographies	geography	graphing	photographs
autobiographical	graphic	graphite	polygraphs
biographies	graphics	orthography	telegraph

www.dynamicliteracy.com

Morpheme Mania

Prefixes

poly   tele   para

auto

Suffixes

ic   er   y   al

ed   s

graph
something written, drawn, or recorded;
chart

Words & Definitions

autographed – wrote one's own signature

Synonyms

signed

Antonyms

copied

Roots

bio   phono   photo   geo

Other

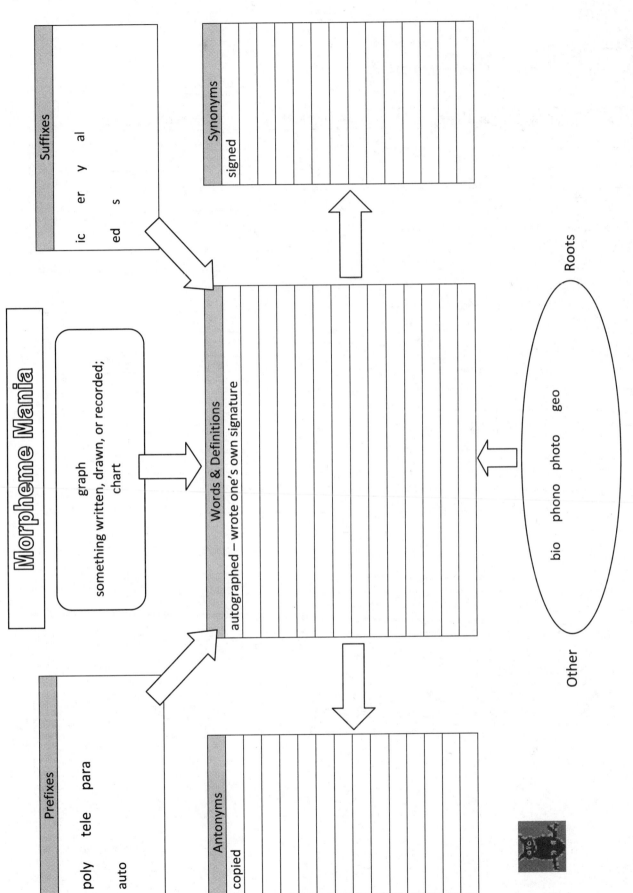

Build as many words as you can for this root family. Use the prefixes and suffixes listed, or add your own. If you use any "combining roots", add them to the "Other Roots" box. Try to think of an antonym and a synonym for each word you build.

My Word Wall

Name _____

Root: *graph*

Word	Synonym / Antonym	Word	Synonym / Antonym

Morphemes for this meaning family

Prefixes	Roots	Suffixes

Root Squares

Name

How many words can you make?

Start in any square. Your goal is to combine two or more word parts to make as many words in the 'lect, leg, lege, legi, lig' family as you can. Write each word and the definition you can think of for it in the space provided at the bottom of the page. Use the back of the page if you need to.

e	ent	di
col	lect, leg, lege, legi, lig	ion
ure	ive	se

Magic Squares

Name _____

Select the best answer for each of the words in the 'lect, leg, lege, legi, lig' family from the numbered definitions. Put the number in the proper space in the Magic Square box. If the total of the numbers is the same both across and down, you have found the magic number!

'lect, leg, lege, legi, lig' means to choose, read, gather, take from

WORDS	DEFINITIONS
A. collections	1. not able to be selected from; not fit or desirable
B. electives	2. things that have been gathered together; assemblies or compilations
C. diligently	3. in a manner able to be read
D. illegible	4. in a manner of choosing apart; in a manner carefully picking out
E. selectively	5. quality of being chosen from; refinement or beauty
F. lecturer	6. not able to be read
G. elector	7. in a manner of choosing apart; in a persevering manner
H. elegance	8. a person reading a chosen text; a person who explains or scolds
I. legibly	9. courses chosen from a list
	10. a person who chooses from; a person chosen to vote someone into office

Magic Square Box

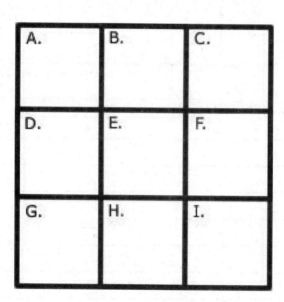

Magic Number ____

Stair Steps

Name

Fill in the missing letters of each 'lect, leg, lege, legi, lig' word by using the definitions below
'lect, leg, lege, legi, lig' means to choose, read, gather, take from

1. | | | l | e | c | t |
2. l | e | g | | | |
3. | l | e | c | t | | |
4. l | e | c | t | | |
5. | | l | e | c | t | |
6. | l | e | c | t | | |
7. | | l | e | c | t | |
8. | | | l | i | g | |

1. to choose apart; to pick out
2. able to be read
3. the process of choosing from; act of voting into office
4. people reading chosen texts; people who explain or scold
5. that which has been gathered together; an assembly or compilation
6. in a manner of choosing apart; in a manner carefully picking out
7. in a manner of being gathered together; in a manner considered as one group
8. inability to be selected from; the lack of fitness or desirability

www.dynamicliteracy.com

The Job at the Museum

In the summer Merle could be found studying <u>in a persevering manner</u> the recent additions to the museum's <u>assembly of documents gathered together</u>. During the school year, Merle had taken a <u>chosen</u> class about old handwritten manuscripts, and he was eager to apply that knowledge to the <u>chosen quality</u> of the <u>items chosen apart</u> that the museum had bought.

Merle remembered that the <u>person reading to the class </u>stressed the importance of wearing white cotton gloves when handling documents to prevent making anything <u>unreadable</u> with oily fingerprints smudges. Merle soon had a reputation of being the most <u>persevering</u> of the museum aides and he was <u>chosen out</u> to guide a weekly tour to look at the prized manuscripts.

Fill in the blanks below using words from the "lect, leg, lege, legi, lig" family.

1. The eager student _____ studied over the manuscripts.

2. The museum's manuscript _____ was quite large and valuable.

3. _____ classes are ones that students can choose.

4. The _____ and the beauty of the manuscripts attracted visitors.

5. Visitors could make _____ about which rooms they wanted to see.

6. The _____ of the class stressed care and cleanliness with the students.

7. We would not want the handwriting to become _____ by smudges.

8. Merle was considered a very _____ student.

9. He was _____ to be a tour guide for the museum.

Word Bank

collection	diligently	elegance	legibility
collectively	elected	illegible	legion
diligent	elective	lecturer	selections

www.dynamicliteracy.com

Morpheme Mania

Prefixes

col   se   e

di

in   il

lect, leg, lege, legi, lig
to choose, read, gather, take from

Suffixes

ent   ion   ure   ive   al

ly   er   ed   ing   s

Words & Definitions

elective – pertaining to choosing from

Synonyms

voluntary

Antonyms

required

Other

Roots

Build as many words as you can for this root family. Use the prefixes and suffixes listed, or add your own. If you use any "combining roots", add them to the "Other Roots" box. Try to think of an antonym and a synonym for each word you build.

www.DynamicLiteracy.com

Root: *lect, leg, lege, legi, lig*

Word	Synonym / Antonym	Word	Synonym / Antonym

Morphemes for this meaning family

Prefixes	Roots	Suffixes

www.dynamicliteracy.com

Root Squares

Name

How many words can you make?

Start in any square. Your goal is to combine two or more word parts to make as many words in the 'equ, equi, eg' family as you can. Write each word and the definition you can think of for it in the space provided at the bottom of the page. Use the back of the page if you need to.

in	ize	ad
al	equ, equi, eg	ate
ity	ion	later

_____

_____

_____

_____

_____

_____

_____

_____

_____

_____

_____

_____

Magic Squares

Name

Select the best answer for each of the words in the 'equ, equi, eg' family from the numbered definitions. Put the number in the proper space in the Magic Square box. If the total of the numbers is the same both across and down, you have found the magic number!

'equ, equi, eg' means fair, balanced

WORDS	DEFINITIONS
A. adequately	1. the state of being unfair and unbalanced
B. equalization	2. the act of making balanced
C. equator	3. state of being balanced, just, or fair
D. inequities	4. conditions in which things are out of balance; acts of unfairness
E. equivalents	5. balanced-sided figures
F. equidistances	6. features of being even in worth
G. equilaterals	7. imaginary line dividing earth into even halves
H. unequaled	8. qualities of standing at a balanced space away from
I. equity	9. in a manner brought to balance or fairness; sufficiently
	10. not of the same fairness and balance; without a peer

Magic Square Box

A.	B.	C.
D.	E.	F.
G.	H.	I.

Magic Number ____

www.dynamicliteracy.com

Stair Steps

Name

Fill in the missing letters of each 'equ, equi, eg' word by using the definitions below
'equ, equi, eg' means fair, balanced

1. | e | q | u | | | |

2. | e | q | u | | | | |

3. | e | q | u | | | | | |

4. | e | q | u | | | | | | |

5. | | | | | e | q | u | | | |

6. | e | q | u | i | | | | | | | |

7. | | | e | q | u | | | | | | | |

8. | e | q | u | i | | | | | | | | | |

1. to make or be fair and balanced; is the same as
2. made even or balanced; showed similarities
3. to balance
4. balanced statements
5. not being brought to balance or fairness; not enough
6. standing at a balanced space away from
7. states of unfairness and imbalance
8. in a way of having balanced sides

Rosa Parks

When Rosa Parks wearily climbed the steps of the bus home from work, she did not realize that she was about to fuel a fight against <u>states of being unfair and unbalanced</u> between the races in Montgomery, Alabama. She wasn't thinking of the <u>unfairness</u> in treatment of blacks and whites; she wasn't thinking of the schools <u>not brought to balance or fairness</u> that black children attended in her city. She was simply tired and heading home. Her refusal to move to back of the bus to seats intended for blacks ignited a struggle for <u>fair and balanced</u> opportunities for all people regardless of race.

In the years since Parks' stand for <u>the state of being balanced and just</u>, laws have been passed and attitudes have changed which have begun to <u>balance</u> opportunities for everyone. More recent movements toward <u>a state of balance</u> among diverse groups, as well as attitudes treating all people <u>in a manner fair and balanced</u> are able to trace their history back to this woman.

Fill in the blanks below using words from the "equ, equi, eg" family.

1. Rosa Parks' actions illustrated one of many _____ between blacks and whites.

2. The segregation of bus seats showed the _____ of the treatment of black and white riders of the bus.

3. In Montgomery, schools for black children were _____ compared to schools for white children.

4. During this time in American history, the chances for every individual to succeed were not _____.

5. Laws were passed to assure that there was _____ for all people.

6. Changes in laws and attitudes served to _____ the circumstances between the races.

7. Society is more secure when an _____ is found among diverse groups.

8. All people deserve to be treated _____ in their pursuits of life, liberty, and happiness.

Word Bank

equal	equalize	inequality	equity
equalities	equate	equilibrium	inadequate
equalization	equatorial	equitably	inequity

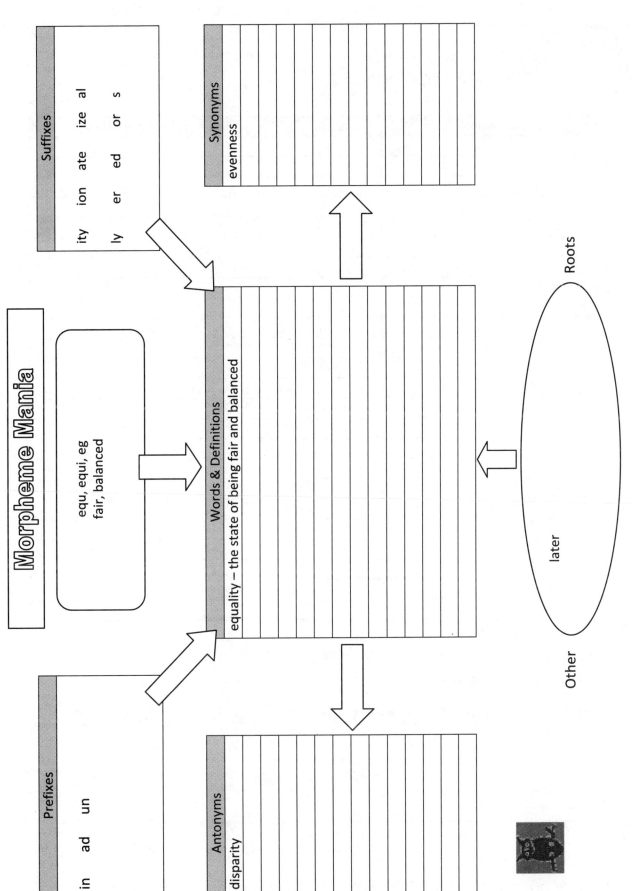

Morpheme Mania

Prefixes

in   ad   un

equ, equi, eg
fair, balanced

Suffixes

ity   ion   ate   ize   al

ly   er   ed   or   s

Words & Definitions

equality – the state of being fair and balanced

Synonyms

evenness

Antonyms

disparity

Roots

later

Other

Build as many words as you can for this root family. Use the prefixes and suffixes listed, or add your own. If you use any "combining roots", add them to the "Other Roots" box. Try to think of an antonym and a synonym for each word you build.

www.DynamicLiteracy.com

My Word Wall

_____
Name

Root: *equ, equi, eg*

Word	Synonym / Antonym	Word	Synonym / Antonym

Morphemes for this meaning family

Prefixes	Roots	Suffixes

www.dynamicliteracy.com

Root Squares

How many words can you make?

Start in any square. Your goal is to combine two or more word parts to make as many words in the 'pet, peat, pete' family as you can. Write each word and the definition you can think of for it in the space provided at the bottom of the page. Use the back of the page if you need to.

im	uate	com
it	pet, peat, pete	re
per	ion	uous

_____

_____

_____

_____

_____

_____

_____

_____

_____

_____

_____

Magic Squares

Name _____

Select the best answer for each of the words in the 'pet, peat, pete' family from the numbered definitions. Put the number in the proper space in the Magic Square box. If the total of the numbers is the same both across and down, you have found the magic number!

'pet, peat, pete' means to seek, aim for; rush

WORDS	DEFINITIONS
A. repetitions	1. likely to seek a goal along with others
B. petitioners	2. something that causes a seeking toward; something to whet the taste
C. appetizer	3. aimed to make something last throughout; eternalized
D. repeatedly	4. so as to have aimed for or sought again; over and over
E. competence	5. seeking to last thoroughly; ever-lasting
F. impetuously	6. in a manner rushing onto; in an impulsive and uncontrolled manner
G. perpetual	7. people who seek something
H. perpetuated	8. the ability to seek a goal along with others
I. petition	9. acts of aiming for or seeking again; acts of saying or doing again
	10. a document that seeks something

Magic Square Box

A.	B.	C.
D.	E.	F.
G.	H.	I.

Magic Number _____

www.dynamicliteracy.com

Stair Steps

Name

Fill in the missing letters of each 'pet, peat, pete' word by using the definitions below
'pet, peat, pete' means to seek, aim for; rush

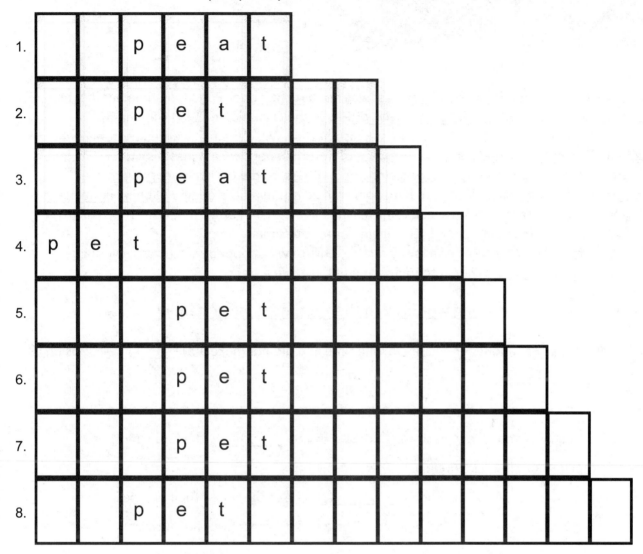

1.   p   e   a   t

2.   p   e   t

3.   p   e   a   t

4. p   e   t

5.   p   e   t

6.   p   e   t

7.   p   e   t

8.   p   e   t

1. to aim for or seek again; to say or do again
2. process of seeking toward; something hungered or yearned for
3. people or tools that aim for or seek again
4. a person who seeks something
5. aimed to make something last throughout; eternalized
6. aiming to make something last throughout; eternalizing
7. in a manner likely to seek goals along with others
8. quality of aiming for or seeking again; quality of being done again and again

Champion Gymnast

Christa's decision to train as a gymnast was not a <u>rushed</u> one. For a long time her idol had been Mary Lou Retton, who <u>sought along with others</u> in the Olympics in 1984, winning the women's gold medal in the All Around. Christa, also born in West Virginia, wanted <u>thoroughly to seek to make everlasting</u> the championship ways of Retton in her own gymnastics career. As her skills grew <u>in a manner likely to seek goals along with others</u>, so did Christa's <u>yearning to seek toward</u> winning. She was dedicated to her sport and did not mind the <u>quality of being done again and again</u> that practice sessions seemed to have. She knew that in order to learn a new skill in floor exercise, she had to <u>aim for and seek again</u> her routines many times.

One afternoon at the end of a long practice, Christa was stopped by a group of young girls <u>seeking in documentary form</u> her autograph. She felt just like a star.

<u>Fill in the blanks below using words from the "pet, peat, pete" family</u>.

1. Christa thought about her decision a long time and did not make a(n) _____ decision to be a gymnast.

2. Mary Lou Retton _____ against women from all over the world in the 1984 Olympics.

3. Becoming a champion gymnast was Christa's way to _____ the fame of other Olympians born in West Virginia.

4. Both Christa and Mary Lou worked _____ to be at the top of their abilities.

5. With a strong _____ for winning, Christa could almost taste her success.

6. To learn the basics, Christa endured the endless _____ of practice sessions.

7. In order to perfect the dismount of her floor exercise, Christa had to _____ it many times.

8. Christa was proud of her hard work when she saw the group of girls _____ for her autograph.

<u>Word Bank</u>

appetite	competitively	incompetency	repeat
appetizer	competitor	perpetuate	repeatedly
competed	impetuous	petitioning	repetitiveness

     www.dynamicliteracy.com

Morpheme Mania

Prefixes

im com re per

ap

pet, peat, pete
to seek, aim for; rush

Suffixes

uate ion it uous

ent ize ive ed s

Words & Definitions

competitive – likely to seek a goal with others

Synonyms

ambitious

Antonyms

cooperative

Roots

Other

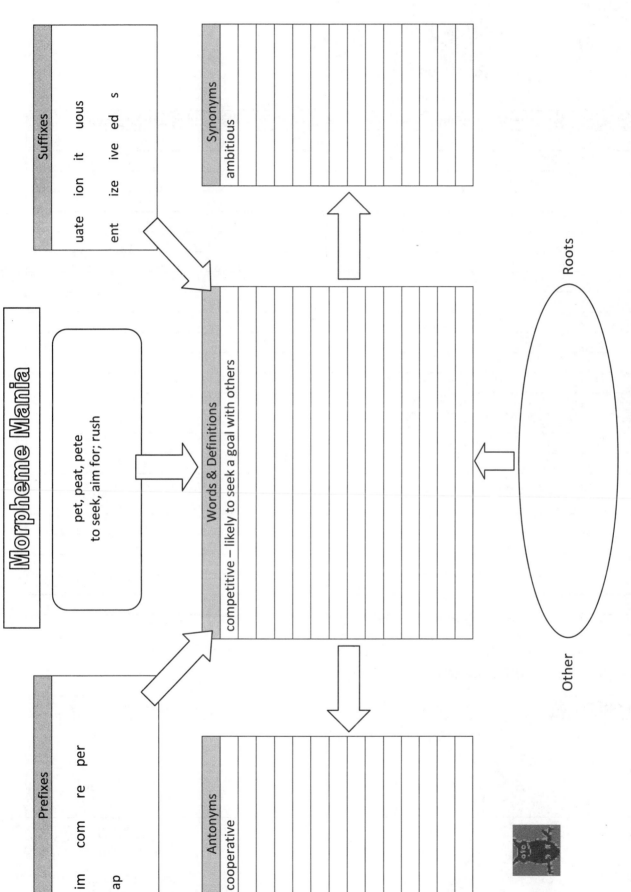

Build as many words as you can for this root family. Use the prefixes and suffixes listed, or add your own. If you use any "combining roots", add them to the "Other Roots" box. Try to think of an antonym and a synonym for each word you build.

www.DynamicLiteracy.com

My Word Wall

Root: *pet, peat, pete*

Word	Synonym / Antonym	Word	Synonym / Antonym

Morphemes for this meaning family

Prefixes	Roots	Suffixes

www.dynamicliteracy.com

Root Squares

Name

How many words can you make?

Start in any square. Your goal is to combine two or more word parts to make as many words in the 'fund, fus, fuse, found' family as you can. Write each word and the definition you can think of for it in the space provided at the bottom of the page. Use the back of the page if you need to.

pro	con	ness
ion	fund, fus, fuse, found	dif
trans	in	ef

www.dynamicliteracy.com

Magic Squares

Name _____

Select the best answer for each of the words in the 'fund, fus, fuse, found' family from the numbered definitions. Put the number in the proper space in the Magic Square box. If the total of the numbers is the same both across and down, you have found the magic number!

'fund, fus, fuse, found' means to melt, pour, or blend

WORDS		DEFINITIONS
A.	transfusing	1. acts of melting and pouring together
B.	refused	2. acts or processes of being blended together; states of perplexity or bewilderment
C.	profusely	3. pouring across; carrying over or penetrating
D.	confounding	4. pouring together; baffling or ruining
E.	confusions	5. in a manner pouring forth; abundantly
F.	diffusion	6. poured into; instilled or permeated
G.	effusions	7. poured back; rejected or was unwilling to accept
H.	infused	8. out-pourings
I.	fusions	9. act of melting or pouring apart; act of scattering or making widespread

Magic Square Box

A.	B.	C.
D.	E.	F.
G.	H.	I.

Magic Number ____

Stair Steps

Name

Fill in the missing letters of each 'fund, fus, fuse, found' word by using the definitions below
'fund, fus, fuse, found' means to melt, pour, or blend

1. | f | u | s | | |
2. | f | u | s | | | |
3. | | | f | u | s | | |
4. | | | | f | u | s | | |
5. | | | | f | u | s | | | |
6. | | | | f | o | u | n | d | | |
7. | | | | f | u | s | e | | | | |
8. | | | | | | f | u | s | | | | |

1. melted and poured together
2. act of melting and pouring together
3. act of pouring back; act of rejecting or not accepting
4. blended together; perplexed or bewildered
5. acts of pouring into; acts of instilling or permeating
6. poured together; baffled or ruined
7. condition of pouring forth; abundance
8. acts of pouring across; processes of carrying over or penetrating

www.dynamicliteracy.com

All Together Now....

The latest thing in music, food, and dance is the <u>act of melting and pouring together</u>. When it comes to food, people used to be afraid <u>to blend together</u> ingredients from different countries. Now, chefs <u>pour forth abundantly</u> such combinations. Herbs and spices that were once <u>poured apart</u> are now <u>poured into</u> one another. It is now common to <u>pour across</u> Caribbean meats with African spices. Such <u>out-pourings</u> are generally well received.

Music is another area where such <u>acts of melting and pouring</u> together are taking place. The influences of musicians from Asia, Europe, and the Americas have provided an <u>act of pouring into</u> music the cultures of many countries.

Was this explanation was not <u>blending together in a manner perplexing or bewildering</u> to you?

Fill in the blanks below using words from the "fund, fus, fuse, found" family.

1. The new style of blending ingredients is called _____.

2. Chefs used to be afraid to _____ ingredients.

3. Now, chefs blend foods from different countries _____.

4. Many _____ ingredients are used with regularity.

5. The result is meals _____ with many flavors.

6. In the cooking process chefs _____ meats with a variety of spices.

7. Such out-pourings, or _____ of flavor are often well received.

8. Music is another area where _____ take place.

9. The _____ of one sound into another creates new and interesting music.

10. If this explanation was _____ to you, you need to study this root a little harder!

Word Bank

profusely	infusion	infused	transfuse
effusions	confuse	fusion	confusing
fusions	profusion	diffuse	confounded

www.dynamicliteracy.com

Morpheme Mania

Prefixes

pro   con   in   dif

trans   ef   re

Suffixes

ness   ion   ed   ry

ing   s   ly

fund, fus, fuse, found
to melt, pour, or blend

Words & Definitions

confuse – to blend together, to bewilder

Synonyms

disorient

Antonyms

clarify

Roots

Other

Build as many words as you can for this root family. Use the prefixes and suffixes listed, <u>or add your own.</u> If you use any "combining roots", add them to the "Other Roots" box. Try to think of an antonym and a synonym for each word you build.

www.DynamicLiteracy.com

Root: *fund, fus, fuse, found*

Word	Synonym / Antonym	Word	Synonym / Antonym

Morphemes for this meaning family

Prefixes	Roots	Suffixes

www.dynamicliteracy.com

Root Squares

Name

How many words can you make?

Start in any square. Your goal is to combine two or more word parts to make as many words in the 'meter, metr' family as you can. Write each word and the definition you can think of for it in the space provided at the bottom of the page. Use the back of the page if you need to.

a	ic	sym
y	**meter, metr**	dia
al	peri	milli

Magic Squares

Select the best answer for each of the words in the 'meter, metr' family from the numbered definitions. Put the number in the proper space in the Magic Square box. If the total of the numbers is the same both across and down, you have found the magic number!

'meter, metr' means measure

WORDS	DEFINITIONS
A. thermometers	1. related to measure through; exactly opposite or contrary
B. symmetrical	2. multiples of 1/1000 of a basic measure of length
C. speedometer	3. devices for measuring heat
D. perimeters	4. measurements around; lengths of boundaries around closed figures
E. millimeters	5. device for measuring velocity
F. metrical	6. in a manner not measuring with; in an uneven or out of proportion manner
G. geometry	7. measuring with; even or in proportion
H. asymmetrically	8. science of measuring the earth; math dealing with area, space, and volume
I. diametrical	9. relating to a system of measurement; relating to units of ten

Magic Square Box

A.	B.	C.
D.	E.	F.
G.	H.	I.

Magic Number ____

Stair Steps

Fill in the missing letters of each 'meter, metr' word by using the definitions below
'meter, metr' means measure

1. | m | e | t | r | | |
2. | m | e | t | e | r | |
3. | | | | m | e | t | e | r |
4. | | | | | m | e | t | e | r |
5. | | | | | m | e | t | r |
6. | | | | | | m | e | t | e | r |
7. | | | | | | | m | e | t | e | r |
8. | | | | m | e | t | r |
9. | | | | | m | e | t | r |

1. relating to a system of measurement; a method of measurement using units of ten
2. measured
3. the measure through; the distance through the centerpoint of a circle
4. the measure around; the length of the boundary around a closed figure
5. not measuring with; uneven or out of proportion
6. multiples of 1/1000 of a basic measure of length
7. devices for measuring velocity
8. so as to measure through; in a manner being exactly opposite or contrary
9. in a manner not measuring with; in an uneven or out of proportion manner

Measurement All Around Us

Note for a moment all the things in your day that are measured:

Before you decide how you'll dress for the day, you might check the temperature on the <u>device for measuring heat</u>. You calculate the <u>measure all the way around</u> of a big-screen TV to see if it will fit on your bedroom wall.

You could read on the carton whether a gallon of milk is in standard measure or <u>a system of measurement using units of ten</u>. Your favorite music has patterned rhythmic <u>measures</u>.

You use <u>math measuring area, space, and volume</u> when you play pool. Is the <u>measure through the middle</u> of a paper towel tube large enough to accommodate a ping-pong ball?

Your home's electricity use is mechanically <u>measured</u> so that you can pay the bill.

You'll get a ticket if you don't watch the <u>device for measuring speed</u> in the car.

You can even describe a sculpture as <u>measured with even proportion</u> or <u>not measured with even proportion</u>, depending on how the parts are arranged.

Fill in the blanks below using words from the "meter, metr" family.

1. Local weathermen use a _____ to report the day's high temperature.

2. Adding up the lengths of all the sides gives you a figure's _____.

3. In contrast to standard measure used in the U.S., most Europeans take measurements using the _____ system that is based on tens.

4. The _____ of music or poetry is its pattern of rhythm.

5. Good pool players study the _____ of the shot to hit at correct angles.

6. The _____ of a circle divides it into two equal parts.

7. The amount of electricity and water have been _____ outside your house.

8. A _____ measures the speed of a moving vehicle.

9. A mirror image, something exactly the same on both sides is described as _____, while a figure that is not the same on both sides is called _____.

Word Bank

asymmetric	geometry	metric	speedometer
barometer	meter	optometrist	symmetrical
diameter	metered	perimeter	thermometer

www.dynamicliteracy.com

Morpheme Mania

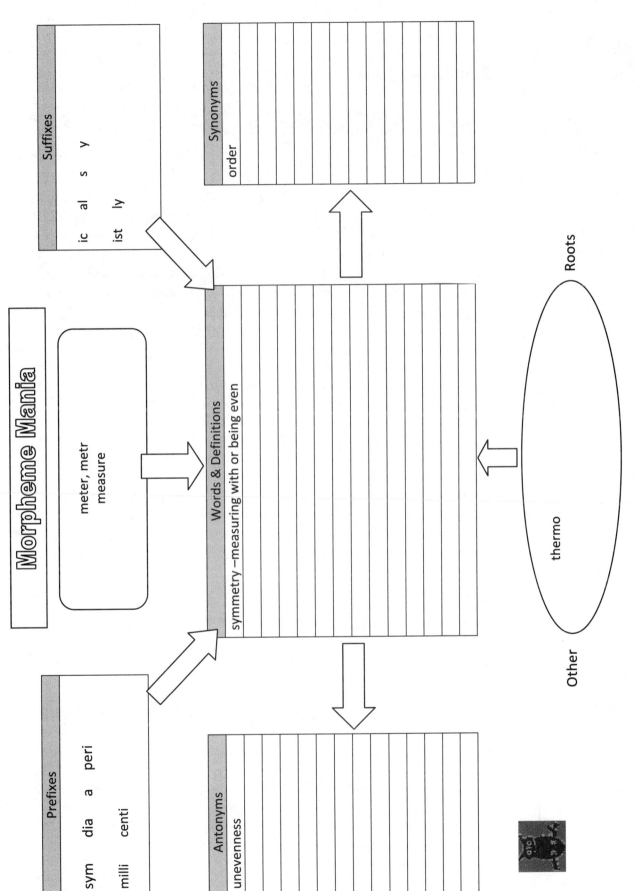

Prefixes

sym　dia　a　peri

milli　centi

Suffixes

ic　al　s　y

ist　ly

meter, metr
measure

Words & Definitions

symmetry –measuring with or being even

Synonyms

order

Antonyms

unevenness

Roots

thermo

Other

Build as many words as you can for this root family. Use the prefixes and suffixes listed, or add your own. If you use any "combining roots", add them to the "Other Roots" box. Try to think of an antonym and a synonym for each word you build.

www.DynamicLiteracy.com

My Word Wall

Root: *meter, metr*

Word	Synonym / Antonym	Word	Synonym / Antonym

Morphemes for this meaning family

Prefixes	Roots	Suffixes

　　　　www.dynamicliteracy.com

Root Squares

How many words can you make?

Start in any square. Your goal is to combine two or more word parts to make as many words in the 'part, parti' family as you can. Write each word and the definition you can think of for it in the space provided at the bottom of the page. Use the back of the page if you need to.

a	com	counter
ure	part, parti	im
ment	ial	de

www.dynamicliteracy.com

Magic Squares

Select the best answer for each of the words in the 'part, parti' family from the numbered definitions. Put the number in the proper space in the Magic Square box. If the total of the numbers is the same both across and down, you have found the magic number!

'part, parti' means side; portion; make a division

WORDS	DEFINITIONS
A. partitioned	1. act of making a division from; a going away
B. counterpart	2. quality of not taking a side; neutrality
C. apartment	3. divided into portions or sides; put a wall between
D. imparting	4. putting a portion into; bestowing ownership to a segment of something
E. participants	5. a portion opposite; a mirror image
F. impartiality	6. involving only one side or portion; incompletely
G. departments	7. a room to the side of the main dwelling
H. departure	8. portions divided off from the whole; distinct subdivisions
I. partially	9. people who share a portion, side, or role

Magic Square Box

A.	B.	C.
D.	E.	F.
G.	H.	I.

Magic Number ____

Stair Steps

Fill in the missing letters of each 'part, parti' word by using the definitions below
'part, parti' means side; piece; make a division

1. | | p | a | r | t |
2. | | | p | a | r | t |
3. | p | a | r | t | | |
4. | | | p | a | r | t | |
5. | | | p | a | r | t | | |
6. | | p | a | r | t | | | |
7. | | | p | a | r | t | | |
8. | | | | | | p | a | r | t | |
9. | p | a | r | t | i | | | | | | | |

1. to the side; not together with the rest
2. to put a piece into; to grant or bestow
3. referring to a piece; incomplete
4. put a piece into; granted or bestowed
5. making a division from; leaving
6. rooms to the side of the main dwelling
7. an area divided off thoroughly; a box or cubbyhole
8. models on the opposite side; mirror images
9. act of taking a side or role

www.dynamicliteracy.com

113

The Big Spell-Off

The top spellers from Canada and their United States <u>mirror images</u> were about to be <u>people who take a role</u> in the North American English Spell-Off. The <u>act of taking a role</u> in this contest was a great honor. A judge and word-caller <u>not taking a side</u> were the officials from Mexico.

The spelling coaches <u>bestowed</u> some last-minute instructions and advice, and then sat <u>to the side</u> away from the spellers. A <u>dividing wall</u> was placed between every competitor so they wouldn't distract each other. One of the prizes was a <u>piece of</u> payment for college expenses.

After an hour of tight competition, the winning word was *compartmentalized*. The winner won <u>in one way</u> because of knowing the six morphemes in the winning word.

Fill in the blanks below using words from the "part, parti" family.

1.   The Canadian spellers greeted their American _____ at the opening ceremony.

2.   All of the _____ of the Spell-Off were champions from their schools.

3.   _____ in such a major event was a great honor.

4.   The judge and caller were _____ and showed favor to neither group.

5.   The coaches _____ some last-minute advice to their spellers.

6.   Then the coaches sat _____ from the spellers.

7.   For better concentration, a _____ was put between every contestant.

8.   _____ payment for future college costs was one of the prizes.

9.   The winning student got the word right _____ by knowing morphemes.

Word Bank

apart	departments	impartially	participation
partition	imparted	partial	compartmentalized
counterparts	impartial	participants	partly

www.dynamicliteracy.com

Morpheme Mania

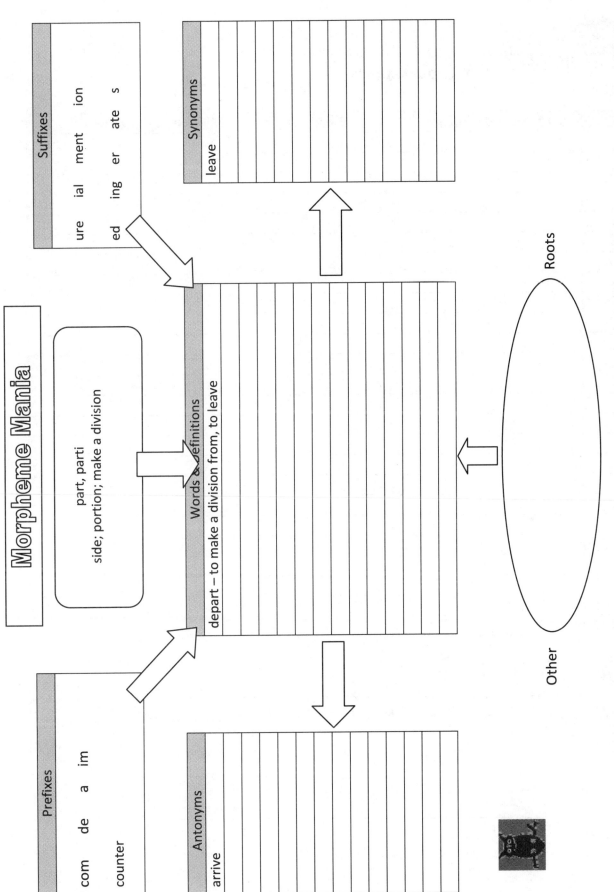

Prefixes

com   de   a   im

counter

Suffixes

ure   ial   ment   ion

ed   ing   er   ate   s

part, parti

side; portion; make a division

Words & Definitions

depart – to make a division from, to leave

Synonyms

leave

Antonyms

arrive

Roots

Other

Build as many words as you can for this root family. Use the prefixes and suffixes listed, or add your own. If you use any "combining roots", add them to the "Other Roots" box. Try to think of an antonym and a synonym for each word you build.

www.DynamicLiteracy.com

Root: *part, parti*

Word	Synonym / Antonym	Word	Synonym / Antonym

Morphemes for this meaning family

Prefixes	Roots	Suffixes

www.dynamicliteracy.com

Root Squares

Name

How many words can you make?

Start in any square. Your goal is to combine two or more word parts to make as many words in the 'lat, late' family as you can. Write each word and the definition you can think of for it in the space provided at the bottom of the page. Use the back of the page if you need to.

cor	re	or
ing	lat, late	ive
trans	ed	e

_____

_____

_____

_____

_____

_____

_____

_____

_____

_____

Copyright Dynamic Literacy, LLC   www.dynamicliteracy.com

117

Magic Squares

Select the best answer for each of the words in the 'lat, late' family from the numbered definitions. Put the number in the proper space in the Magic Square box. If the total of the numbers is the same both across and down, you have found the magic number!

'lat, late' means to bring

WORDS

A. translators
B. superlatively
C. relatively
D. relations
E. elating
F. dilated
G. correlation
H. translating
I. legislate

DEFINITIONS

1. a person who brings across; a person who puts works into a different language
2. in a manner brought above; so as to be the best in the category
3. act of bringing back together; quality of meshing or being similar
4. brought apart; widened or expanded
5. to bring into law; to enact law
6. bringing out; making very happy
7. people who bring across; people who put works into a different language
8. acts of bringing back; acts of telling stories or of fitting in
9. in a manner that brings back; with respect to being compared
10. bringing across; putting into a different language

Magic Square Box

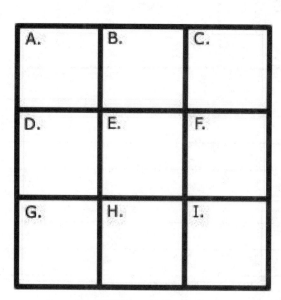

Magic Number _____

www.dynamicliteracy.com

Stair Steps

Name _____

Fill in the missing letters of each 'lat, late' word by using the definitions below
'lat, late' means to bring

1. | | l | a | t | e |
2. | | l | a | t | e |
3. | l | a | t | |
4. | l | a | t | |
5. | l | a | t | e |
6. | l | a | t | |
7. | l | a | t | |
8. | l | a | t | |
9. | l | a | t | |

1. to bring out; to make very happy
2. to bring back; to tell a story or to fit in
3. bringing out; making very happy
4. acts of being brought out; states of being very happy
5. to bring across; to put into a different language
6. in a manner that brings back; with respect to being compared
7. act of bringing back together; quality of meshing or being similar
8. acts or processes of bringing across; works put into a different language
9. in a manner brought above; so as to be the best in the category

www.dynamicliteracy.com

Einstein

The eyes of most of us are <u>brought apart</u> with wonder and amazement about two ideas that Albert Einstein figured out. One is the theory of <u>comparison</u>. One simple way to understand that is to think of yourself walking forward at three miles per hour on a bus that is moving 50 miles per hour. <u>Brought</u> back in comparison to the ground, you are actually walking 53 miles per hour.

Einstein's famous formula, e=mc^2, <u>is brought across</u> into the words "energy equals mass times the speed of light squared." This means that energy, mass, and light <u>are brought back together</u> in a comparison. Although this opened the way to develop nuclear weapons, Einstein was always interested in national <u>law-bringing</u> against such weapons.

If you've ever thought you weren't as smart as somebody else, you might be <u>brought out of yourself with happiness</u> to know that Einstein, with an intellect most <u>brought above in comparison</u> of all time, was considered dull by some of his early teachers. A story is <u>brought back</u> that this genius failed some of his subjects in school.

It just goes to show that there is not necessarily a <u>quality of being brought back together</u> between early performance and later achievement.

Fill in the blanks below using words from the "lat, late" family.

1.   When the pupils of our eyes get large, they are said to have _____.

2.   The theory of _____ involves a comparison among place, time, and speed.

3.   The _____ speeds of two objects is figured out by adding or subtracting them.

4.   The famous formula _____ into nine simple words.

5.   Energy, mass, and light _____ with each other.

6.   Some nations have enacted _____ that outlaws nuclear weapons.

7.   Many of us are _____ to learn that a weak start doesn't mean a weak finish.

8.   Einstein's intellect is one of the most _____ that the world has ever known.

9.   A story has been _____ that the genius was weak at some school subjects.

10. Sometimes there is no _____ between two events.

Word Bank

correlate	elated	related	superlative
correlations	legislation	relative	translates
dilated	legislator	relativity	translator

www.dynamicliteracy.com

Morpheme Mania

Prefixes

cor   re   e   trans

di

lat, late
to bring

Suffixes

or   ive   ure   ly

ed   ing   s   ion

Words & Definitions

elate – to bring out, to make very happy

Synonyms

overjoy

Antonyms

depress

Roots

legis

Other

Build as many words as you can for this root family. Use the prefixes and suffixes listed, or add your own. If you use any "combining roots", add them to the "Other Roots" box. Try to think of an antonym and a synonym for each word you build.

All rights reserved

www.DynamicLiteracy.com

My Word Wall

Root: *lat, late*

Word	Synonym / Antonym	Word	Synonym / Antonym

Morphemes for this meaning family

Prefixes	Roots	Suffixes

www.dynamicliteracy.com

Root Squares

How many words can you make?

Start in any square. Your goal is to combine two or more word parts to make as many words in the 'vol, volt, volv, volve, volut, volute' family as you can. Write each word and the definition you can think of for it in the space provided at the bottom of the page. Use the back of the page if you need to.

con	ize	re
ary	vol, volt, volv, volve, volut, volute	ist
e	ion	counter

_____

_____

_____

_____

_____

_____

_____

_____

_____

_____

_____

_____

www.dynamicliteracy.com

Magic Squares

Select the best answer for each of the words in the 'vol, volt, volv, volve, volut, volute' family from the numbered definitions. Put the number in the proper space in the Magic Square box. If the total of the numbers is the same both across and down, you have found the magic number!

'vol, volt, volv, volve, volut, volute' means to roll, turn, coil, or fold

WORDS	DEFINITIONS
A. revolving	1. qualities of being coiled or rolled in; qualities of being drawn in or a part of
B. revolutionizing	2. rolling back; rising up against forcefully
C. revolters	3. rolling back the old for new
D. involvements	4. able to roll again; able circle around a set point
E. evolved	5. people who roll back; people who rise up against forcefully
F. devolving	6. people against overturning the old for the new
G. convoluted	7. aiming to roll back the old for the new
H. counterrevolutionists	8. rolled out; developed
I. revolvable	9. rolling again; circling around a set point
	10. a person who believes in a rolling out; a person who believes in a gradual progressio
	11. rolled together; complicated; mixed up and intricate
	12. rolling down; passing down to

Magic Square Box

A.	B.	C.
D.	E.	F.
G.	H.	I.

Magic Number ____

Stair Steps

Name

Fill in the missing letters of each 'vol, volt, volv, volve, volut, volute' word by using the definitions
'vol, volt, volv, volve, volut, volute' means to roll, turn, coil, or fold

1.		v	o	l	v	e
2.			v	o	l	v	e
3.			v	o	l	v	e
4.		v	o	l	u	t
5.			v	o	l	v
6.			v	o	l	v	e
7.		v	o	l	u	t
8.			v	o	l	u	t
9.			v	o	l	u	t

1. to roll out; to develop
2. to roll again; to circle around a set point
3. coils or rolls in; concerns or includes
4. act or process of rolling out; a gradual maturing or progress
5. able to roll again; able circle around a set point
6. quality of being coiled or rolled in; quality of being drawn in or a part of
7. marked by rolling out; marked by gradually maturing or progressing
8. a person aiming to roll back the old for the new
9. aimed to roll back the old for the new

 **In Other Words...**

Name

Sorry, Pluto.....

Scientific theory constantly <u>rolls out and develops</u> as more information is learned. Recently, scientists declared that our solar system was one planet short of the nine that science books taught. This was enough to cause a <u>forceful rise up against</u> the decision in classrooms across the country. What was the reasoning behind "deplaneting" the smallest and most remote of the bodies that <u>roll around the set point</u> of our sun? Did the reasoning <u>concern</u> the planet's orbit? Was it that Pluto's <u>act or process of rolling around</u> was erratic? Did the planet's rocks <u>pass</u> down into wispy clouds and disappear?

This last step in Pluto's <u>gradual progress</u> from planet, originally discovered in 1930, to "dwarf planet" occurred in August, 2006. Scientists agreed that one major characteristic of a planet was that it sweeps smaller objects clean from the region immediately around it. Since Pluto occupies a region that contains a lot of other small objects in its space, it cannot be a planet.

Of course there are dissenters who say Pluto **is** a planet. Is there a <u>movement against overthrowing the old for the new</u> on the horizon?

Fill in the blanks below using words from the "vol, volt, volv, volve, volut" family.

1. Scientific ideas change over time and theory _____ as more information is gathered and analyzed.

2. Some classrooms that were obviously fans of the small planet staged a _____ in their science classrooms to protest the decision.

3. Pluto does _____ around the sun just as other planets do.

4. Pluto's removal as a planet did not _____ trouble with its orbit around the sun.

5. There was no dispute about Pluto's _____ on its axis.

6. The solid material comprising Pluto's mass did not _____ into gaseous clouds.

7. Pluto's _____ from planet to dwarf planet took over seventy years.

8. There are scientists who disagree with booting Pluto from the list of planets; their _____ may have it reinstated in the years to come.

Word Bank

convoluted	evolves	involvement	revolutionist
counterrevolution	evolution	revolt	revolve
devolve	involve	revolution	revolver

www.dynamicliteracy.com

Morpheme Mania

Prefixes

con   re   e   counter

trans   in

vol, volt, volv, volve, volut, volute

to roll, turn, coil, or fold

Suffixes

ist   ize   ary   ion

ed   ing   s

Words & Definitions

revolving – rolling again, turning around a point

Synonyms

spinning

Antonyms

stationary

Roots

Other

Build as many words as you can for this root family. Use the prefixes and suffixes listed, or add your own. If you use any "combining roots", add them to the "Other Roots" box. Try to think of an antonym and a synonym for each word you build.

My Word Wall

Name _____

Root: *vol, volt, volv, volve, volut, volute*

Word	Synonym / Antonym	Word	Synonym / Antonym

Morphemes for this meaning family

Prefixes	Roots	Suffixes

Root Squares

Name

How many words can you make?

Start in any square. Your goal is to combine two or more word parts to make as many words in the 'stru, strue, struct' family as you can. Write each word and the definition you can think of for it in the space provided at the bottom of the page. Use the back of the page if you need to.

un	de	ive
infra	stru, strue, struct	con
ure	or	ob

Magic Squares

Name

Select the best answer for each of the words in the 'stru, strue, struct' family from the numbered definitions. Put the number in the proper space in the Magic Square box. If the total of the numbers is the same both across and down, you have found the magic number!

'stru, strue, struct' means to build; arrange; pile up

WORDS	DEFINITIONS
A. constructions	1. helping to build in or arrange; aiding to develop or achieve
B. indestructibly	2. things built or arranged together; things made
C. constructively	3. built or arranged together again; made again
D. instructors	4. parts of buildings within; internal frameworks of buildings
E. infrastructures	5. in a manner related to the basic arrangement of
F. destructive	6. people who build into; teachers
G. unobstructed	7. in a manner serving to build or arrange together; helpfully
H. structurally	8. causing to be unbuilt or disarranged; resulting in ruin or broken parts
I. reconstructed	9. so as not to be capable of being unbuilt or disarranged; in a way not capable of being broken apart
	10. with nothing piled up against; not blocked

Magic Square Box

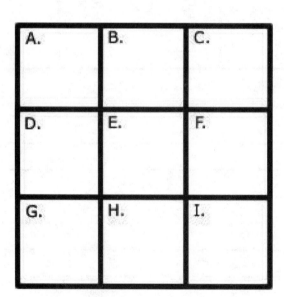

Magic Number ____

www.dynamicliteracy.com

Stair Steps

Name

Fill in the missing letters of each 'stru, strue, struct' word by using the definitions below
'stru, strue, struct' means to build; arrange; pile up

1. | | | s | t | r | u | c | t | |
2. | | | s | t | r | u | c | t | |
3. | s | t | r | u | c | t | | | |
4. | | | | | s | t | r | u | c | t |
5. | | | s | t | r | u | c | t | |
6. | | | s | t | r | u | c | t | |
7. | | | | | s | t | r | u | c | t |

1. to pile up against; to block
2. builds into; teaches
3. related to the basic arrangement of
4. to build or arrange together again; to make again
5. things piled up against; things that block
6. in a manner serving to build into; in a manner serving to teach
7. building or arranging together again; making again

www.dynamicliteracy.com

Building a Birdhouse

Molly decided to build a birdhouse for her 4-H project. Because her uncle was in the <u>building and making</u> business, she had tools. She also had a book <u>for the process of teaching</u> her and blueprints showing measurements for the wood pieces <u>related to the basic arrangement</u> that she needed.

Molly worked quickly to assemble the pieces, but the roof wouldn't fit correctly on top of the birdhouse. She had to <u>undo what had been built together</u> at the front of the house and decided to watch a video <u>serving to build know-how</u>, hoping it would help fix the problem. The video warned to make sure that the entrance to the birdhouse had no <u>things piled up against it</u>, so that the birds could enter.

Later, Molly <u>arranged in her mind</u> that her project was a success when she heard chirping coming from the little house. When she presented the project to her 4-H club, Molly offered to <u>put know-how into</u> anyone wanting to learn about making birdhouses.

<u>Fill in the blanks below using words from the "stru, strue, struct" family</u>.

1. The idea to build a birdhouse was obvious to Molly because her uncle was in the
   _____ business.

2. Assembling the pieces without an _____ booklet would be difficult.

3. Walls, floor and roof make up the _____ pieces for the birdhouse project.

4. When she made a mistake Molly had to _____ part of the building and repair it.

5. Watching an _____ video before starting may have helped Molly arrange the pieces
   correctly the first time.

6. Without _____ at the door of the birdhouse, birds could enter and leave easily.

7. Molly _____ that birds had moved into the house when she heard them chirping.

8. She did such a good job that she could _____ other students in her club on making a
   birdhouse.

<u>Word Bank</u>

construction	destructive	instructive	obstructions
construed	instruct	instrumentally	structural
deconstruct	instruction	obstruct	structured

 www.dynamicliteracy.com

Morpheme Mania

Prefixes

con   un   de   ob

infra   in

stru, strue, struct

to build; arrange; pile up

Suffixes

ive   ure   or   ion

ed   ing   s   ment

Words & Definitions

obstructing – piling up against, blocking

Synonyms

blocking

Antonyms

freeing

Roots

Other

Build as many words as you can for this root family. Use the prefixes and suffixes listed, or add your own. If you use any "combining roots", add them to the "Other Roots" box. Try to think of an antonym and a synonym for each word you build.

www.DynamicLiteracy.com

My Word Wall

Root: *stru, strue, struct*

Word	Synonym / Antonym	Word	Synonym / Antonym

Morphemes for this meaning family

Prefixes	Roots	Suffixes

Root Squares

How many words can you make?

Start in any square. Your goal is to combine two or more word parts to make as many words in the 'spir, spire, spiro, pir, pire' family as you can. Write each word and the definition you can think of for it in the space provided at the bottom of the page. Use the back of the page if you need to.

re	ed	per
ex	spir, spire, spiro, pir, pire	in
a	ant	ion

_____

_____

_____

_____

_____

_____

_____

_____

_____

_____

_____

www.dynamicliteracy.com

Magic Squares

Select the best answer for each of the words in the 'spir, spire, spiro, pir, pire' family from the numbered definitions. Put the number in the proper space in the Magic Square box. If the total of the numbers is the same both across and down, you have found the magic number!

'spir, spire, spiro, pir, pire' means to breathe; to whisper; essence

WORDS	DEFINITIONS
A. aspirations	1. serving to breathe into; relating to motivation and encouragement
B. transpired	2. people whispering with others; people secretly plotting
C. spiritually	3. acts or processes of breathing toward; desires for high goals
D. perspiring	4. breathing through; sweating
E. aspirants	5. breathed through; gave off vapor or occurred
F. conspirators	6. the process of breathing again; the act of breathing in and out
G. expiration	7. so as to pertain to the breath of life; so as to relate to the animating force of life
H. inspirational	
I. respiration	8. act of breathing out; an end
	9. people breathing toward; people desiring high goals

Magic Square Box

A.	B.	C.
D.	E.	F.
G.	H.	I.

Magic Number ____

　www.dynamicliteracy.com

Stair Steps

Name

Fill in the missing letters of each 'spir, spire, spiro, pir, pire' word by using the definitions below
'spir, spire, spiro, pir, pire' means to breathe; to whisper; essence

1. | | | p | i | r | e |
2. | | s | p | i | r | e |
3. | s | p | i | r | | |
4. | | s | p | i | r | e |
5. | p | i | r | | | |
6. | s | p | i | r | | |
7. | s | p | i | r | | |
8. | | s | p | i | r | |

1. to breathe out; to run out of time or end
2. to breathe into; to motivate and encourage
3. breathing toward; desiring a high goal
4. whispers together; secretly plots together
5. act of breathing out; an end
6. act of breathing into; motivation and encouragement
7. act of breathing through; sweat
8. the act of breathing through; process of giving off vapor

Juno Tries to Ruin Hercules

Juno, the Queen of Mt. Olympus, hated Hercules and <u>secretly plotted</u> with others to drive Hercules crazy. She brought it about that Hercules fell into a fit of insanity and unknowingly killed his own children. When Hercules snapped out of his insanity, he saw what had <u>happened</u> and lost all the <u>liveliness and animation</u> from his body.

Hercules <u>breathed toward the high goal</u> to be forgiven for his crimes. <u>Breathed into</u> by a sense of purpose, he became a slave to a king and offered to accomplish whatever tasks might be given to him.

The first task was to squeeze a lion to death. <u>Sweat</u> poured from his body as he wrestled the lion. The rate of his <u>breathing in and out again</u> had tripled. Finally the lion <u>breathed out</u> its last and Hercules was the victor.

Eleven more tasks would <u>occur</u> before it was all over, but finally Hercules was cleansed <u>in a manner relating to his breath</u> of life and sat with the gods on Mt. Olympus.

Fill in the blanks below using words from the "spir, spire, spiro, pir, pire" family.

1. Juno and other enemies of Hercules _____ to bring about his downfall.

2. Hercules was horrified to learn what had _____ while he was in a fit.

3. It was as if his _____ left his body.

4. Hercules _____ toward a high goal.

5. A sense of purpose _____ Hercules to life and become a better person.

6. The _____ poured from Hercules' body as he wrestled.

7. His _____ rate tripled.

8. Even more exhausted than Hercules, the lion finally _____ its last breath.

9. Twelve tasks in all would _____ before the ordeal of Hercules was over.

10. The labors cleansed Hercules _____ and he had a new outlook.

Word Bank

aspirations	conspired	perspiration	spirit
aspired	expired	respiration	spiritually
conspiracy	inspired	transpired	transpire

www.dynamicliteracy.com

Morpheme Mania

Prefixes

re   per   ex   a

in   con   trans

spir, spire, spiro, pir, pire

to breathe; to whisper; essence

Suffixes

at   ion   or   ual

ed   ing   s   it

Words & Definitions

inspire – to breath into, to motivate

Synonyms

encourage

Antonyms

repress

Roots

Other

Build as many words as you can for this root family. Use the prefixes and suffixes listed, or add your own. If you use any "combining roots", add them to the "Other Roots" box. Try to think of an antonym and a synonym for each word you build.

Root: *spir, spire, spiro, pir, pire*

Word	Synonym / Antonym	Word	Synonym / Antonym

Morphemes for this meaning family

Prefixes	Roots	Suffixes

www.dynamicliteracy.com

Root Squares

How many words can you make?

Start in any square. Your goal is to combine two or more word parts to make as many words in the 'man, mann, manu' family as you can. Write each word and the definition you can think of for it in the space provided at the bottom of the page. Use the back of the page if you need to.

age	mis	fact
ment	man, mann, manu	ure
er	script	able

www.dynamicliteracy.com

Magic Squares

Name _____

Select the best answer for each of the words in the 'man, mann, manu' family from the numbered definitions. Put the number in the proper space in the Magic Square box. If the total of the numbers is the same both across and down, you have found the magic number!

'man, mann, manu' means hand

WORDS
A. emancipating
B. manageable
C. mannerly
D. manuscript
E. manufacturers
F. manually
G. unmannered
H. mismanages
I. managers

DEFINITIONS
1. a document written by hand
2. act of taking from the hand; act of liberation from a master
3. uncontrollable, not able to be handled; unable to deal with
4. handles in a bad way
5. handleable; able to be dealt with or controlled
6. people who handle; people who deal with or control
7. having ways of handling things; polite
8. in a manner done by hand
9. taking from the hand; liberating from a master
10. not made by hand; not produced or created
11. marked by a way of not handling something; without a specific method or style
12. people who make products by hand (or machine)

Magic Square Box

A.	B.	C.
D.	E.	F.
G.	H.	I.

Magic Number ____

Stair Steps

Fill in the missing letters of each 'man, mann, manu' word by using the definitions below
'man, mann, manu' means hand

1. | m | a | n | u | | |
2. | m | a | n | n | | |
3. | m | a | n | | | |
4. | | | | m | a | n |
5. | m | a | n | | | |
6. | m | a | n | u | | |
7. | m | a | n | u | | |
8. | | | | m | a | n |

1. related to hands; done by hand
2. ways of handling things; socially accepted habits
3. people who handle; people who deal with or control
4. to handle in a bad way
5. pertaining to handling; related to dealing with or controlling
6. documents written by hand
7. a person who makes products by hand (or machine)
8. quality of handling in a bad way

www.dynamicliteracy.com

Farmer, Writer, and Friend to Raiders

Snorri of Iceland <u>handled</u> his little sheep farm well. He had <u>liberated and taken out from his hand</u> the indentured servant he once had and did all the <u>hand</u> labor himself. He and his wife Bergthora also made a living by the <u>hand-making</u> of sheepskins used for writing. Bergthora was an excellent <u>handler</u> of the estate. Many of their neighbors had <u>badly handled</u> their lands and had become <u>impolite</u>, roving Vikings.

Sometimes when former neighbors came back from a raid, they would stay with Snorri and Bergthora, and they would tell about their adventures. Snorri would put these stories in form <u>written by hand</u>, and these <u>documents written by hand</u> became sources of some famous sagas.

Fill in the blanks below using words from the "man, mann, manu" family.

1. Snorri owned and _____ a little sheep farm in Iceland.

2. He did all the work himself because he had _____ his farmhand.

3. Gathering grass, milking sheep, cutting wool, and other _____ labor kept

4. him busy and tired.

5. Income was also gained by the _____ of sheepskin for writing.

6. Bergthora was an excellent _____ of the estate.

7. Other Icelanders had _____ their lands and failed as farmers.

8. They turned from farming and took up a life as wild, _____ Vikings.

9. Using his sheepskins, Snorri wrote out some stories in _____ form.

10. His _____ are still known for the great stories they tell.

Word Bank

emancipated	manager	manufacture	manuscripts
emancipation	manual	manure	mismanaged
managed	manually	manuscript	unmannerly

www.dynamicliteracy.com

Morpheme Mania

Prefixes

mis   e   un

man, mann, manu

hand

Suffixes

age   ure   er   able   s

ate   ion   ed   ment

Words & Definitions

manual – done by hands

Synonyms

physical

Antonyms

mechanical

Roots

fact   script   cip

Other

Build as many words as you can for this root family. Use the prefixes and suffixes listed, or add your own. If you use any "combining roots", add them to the "Other Roots" box. Try to think of an antonym and a synonym for each word you build.

©2007 Dynamic Literacy, LLC

www.DynamicLiteracy.com

My Word Wall

Root: *man, mann, manu*

Word	Synonym / Antonym	Word	Synonym / Antonym

Morphemes for this meaning family

Prefixes	Roots	Suffixes

www.dynamicliteracy.com

Root Squares

Name

How many words can you make?

Start in any square. Your goal is to combine two or more word parts to make as many words in the 'mem, ment' family as you can. Write each word and the definition you can think of for it in the space provided at the bottom of the page. Use the back of the page if you need to.

de	ed	ize
or	mem, ment	y
al	ity	com

www.dynamicliteracy.com

Magic Squares

Name _____

Select the best answer for each of the words in the 'mem, ment' family from the numbered definitions. Put the number in the proper space in the Magic Square box. If the total of the numbers is the same both across and down, you have found the magic number!

'mem, ment' means mind

WORDS	DEFINITIONS
A. mentor	1. frame of mind; sum of intellectual power
B. mentionable	2. writing or voicing a note to call to mind
C. memorizations	3. a person who guides thinking; a person who counsels a student
D. commemorations	4. acts of bringing something to mind with others
E. commenting	5. acts of committing data to the mind
F. dementia	6. people who write or voice notes to call to mind
G. memorializing	7. able to be brought to mind; able to be said briefly and informally
H. commentators	8. keeping in the mind across time
I. mentality	9. state of being out of one's mind; craziness

Magic Square Box

A.	B.	C.
D.	E.	F.
G.	H.	I.

Magic Number _____

www.dynamicliteracy.com

Stair Steps

Name

Fill in the missing letters of each 'mem, ment' word by using the definitions below
'mem, ment' means mind

1.	m	e	n	t		
2.	m	e	n	t		
3.			m	e	n	t
4.	m	e	m			
5.	m	e	n	t		
6.	m	e	m			
7.			m	e	n	t
8.	m	e	m			
9.			m	e	m	

1. related to the mind
2. people who guide thinking; people who counsel students
3. out of one's mind; crazy
4. commits to the mind in order to recall
5. bringing to mind; saying briefly and informally
6. to keep in the mind across time
7. people who write or voice notes to call to mind
8. keeping in the mind across time
9. acts of bringing something to mind with others

Name _____

Useless, Never-ending Work

King Sisyphus, who thought he was better and smarter than the gods of Greece, once managed to tie up Hades, the god of the underworld, so that nothing on earth would die. This <u>step across in violation</u> against gods and men halted the natural <u>stepping forward</u> of life and death. Even warriors, hacked to bits in battle, would not die, and <u>in slow-step manner</u> the earth became too crowded. Hades finally escaped from Sisyphus' trickery and ordered him to appear in the underworld for punishment.

However, Sisyphus had another trick up his sleeve. Planning in <u>step together</u> with his wife, Sisyphus arranged not to have an official funeral service. When he got to the underworld, he <u>stepped back</u> to childish behavior and begged Queen Persephone to allow him to go home for a proper burial. (Queen Persephone is in the underworld herself as a result of a trick, but we must not <u>step apart</u> from Sisyphus' story.)

Hades grows angry <u>in a manner moving forward</u> with Sisyphus and sentences him to eternal labor. Sisyphus' task is to roll a boulder up a steep hill, a task that he undertakes <u>in a hostile manner</u>, sweat popping from his brow. After he rolls the boulder to the top of the hill, it rolls back down the steep <u>slope</u>. Sisyphus has to start all over again and again forever.

<u>Fill in the blanks below using words from the "grad, grade, gress" family</u>.

1. Sisyphus made some serious _____ against the rules of gods and men.

2. There is a natural _____ in life as we are born, grow up, and pass from earth.

3. _____, earth filled up with too many people.

4. Sisyphus' wife planned in _____ with him how to trick Hades again.

5. In order to sweet-talk the queen, Sisyphus _____ to the habits of a young child.

6. Telling Persephone's story would be to _____ from the story of Sisyphus.

7. Hades' ill will toward Sisyphus piled up as he became _____ angrier.

8. Sisyphus pushes the boulder so _____ that it becomes a tough workout.

9. The steep _____ of the hill made Sisyphus' task even harder.

Word Bank

aggressively	degrading	grader	progressively
centigrade	digress	gradually	regressed
congress	grade	progression	transgression

Morpheme Mania

Prefixes

com   de

mem, ment

mind

Suffixes

ed   ize   or   y   s

al   ity   ing   ial   ia

Words & Definitions

memorizes – commits to the mind

Synonyms

acquires

Antonyms

forgets

Roots

Other

Build as many words as you can for this root family. Use the prefixes and suffixes listed, or add your own. If you use any "combining roots", add them to the "Other Roots" box. Try to think of an antonym and a synonym for each word you build.

www.DynamicLiteracy.com

My Word Wall

Name

Root: *mem, ment*

Word	Synonym / Antonym	Word	Synonym / Antonym

Morphemes for this meaning family

Prefixes	Roots	Suffixes

www.dynamicliteracy.com

Root Squares

Name

How many words can you make?

Start in any square. Your goal is to combine two or more word parts to make as many words in the 'claim, clam, clat' family as you can. Write each word and the definition you can think of for it in the space provided at the bottom of the page. Use the back of the page if you need to.

re	at	ac
ory	claim, clam, clat	ed
pro	ion	ex

_____

_____

_____

_____

_____

_____

_____

_____

_____

_____

_____

_____

Magic Squares

Select the best answer for each of the words in the 'claim, clam, clat' family from the numbered definitions. Put the number in the proper space in the Magic Square box. If the total of the numbers is the same both across and down, you have found the magic number!

'claim, clam, clat' means to demand; call out for; shout

WORDS	DEFINITIONS
A. unclaimed	1. an act or process of shouting forth; an official declaration
B. reclaimable	2. tending to be shouted out; spoken out with sudden or strong emotion
C. proclaimed	3. not called for; not taken into ownership
D. nomenclature	4. a system to call things by name
E. exclamatory	5. shouted forth; declared officially
F. disclaimers	6. the act of shouting toward; the act or process of praising
G. clamorously	7. able to be demanded or asked for again; able to be taken back in ownership
H. acclamation	8. in a manner full of loud shouting; noisily
I. proclamation	9. statements that call out denial; renunciations or acts of disownment

Magic Square Box

A.	B.	C.
D.	**E.**	**F.**
G.	**H.**	**I.**

Magic Number ____

www.dynamicliteracy.com

Stair Steps

Name

Fill in the missing letters of each 'claim, clam, clat' word by using the definitions below
'claim, clam, clat' means to demand; call out for; shout

1. | c | l | a | i | m | |
2. | | | c | l | a | i | m |
3. | c | l | a | i | m |
4. | | | c | l | a | i | m |
5. | | | | c | l | a | i | m |
6. | | | c | l | | a | m |
7. | | | c | l | | a | m |
8. | | | | c | l | | a | m |

1. demands or asks for; states ownership
2. to shout out; to speak out with sudden or strong emotion
3. demanding or asking for; stating ownership
4. demanded or asked for again; took back in ownership
5. a denial or giving up demanding; a renunciation or disownment
6. the act of shouting toward; the act or process of praising
7. acts or processes of shouting out; sudden or emotionally strong statements
8. acts or processes of shouting forth; official declarations

www.dynamicliteracy.com

Rock Concert

"It's the Frogs! The Frogs at the arena," Betsy squealed when she heard the radio announcer <u>shout forth</u> the weekend's entertainment. "I've always wanted to see them perform live," she <u>shouted out</u>. "Pleeeese, Mom, may I go? PLEASE…." she <u>shouted noisily</u>. "They're so great. They <u>are praised</u> internationally. It says so in my fan magazine. I can't miss a group that famous. What if they never tour here again, huh?"

"I thought you might like to go to the concert," Betsy's mother said smiling as she handed her an envelope. "Wow, Mom!" Betsy's <u>act of shouting out</u> could be heard next door at the neighbor's house. "TWO tickets! I'll call Jill."

"Wait a minute, Betts. I'm going with you. How can I miss the famous Frogs with such an interesting <u>system of being named</u>?" her mother asked. "Besides, the <u>denial</u> on the ticket reads that no one under eighteen will be admitted without an adult."

"Oh," Betsy mumbled. "But maybe Jill can get a seat that has <u>not been called for</u>."

Fill in the blanks below using words from the "claim, clam, clat" family.

1. Betsy heard the announcer _____ the Frogs' appearance in her town.

2. "What an opportunity!" the excited girl _____ when she heard the news.

3. Begging her mother, Betsy _____ for tickets to see the group.

4. The Frogs are _____ all over the world.

5. Neighbors knew Betsy won her mom over when they heard her _____ of joy.

6. Her Mom thought the _____ of rock groups was interesting.

7. An age-limit _____ appeared on the concert ticket stub.

8. There might be some _____ seats so that others could attend.

Word Bank

acclaimed	clamorous	exclaimer	proclaim
acclaiming	disclaimer	exclamation	reclaiming
clamored	exclaimed	nomenclature	unclaimed

www.dynamicliteracy.com

Morpheme Mania

Prefixes

pro   re   ex   ac

dis

claim, clam, clat

to demand; call out for; shout

Suffixes

ed   at   ory   ion

er   s   ing

Words & Definitions

disclaims – denies or gives up demanding

Synonyms

renounces

Antonyms

accepts

Other   Roots

Build as many words as you can for this root family. Use the prefixes and suffixes listed, or add your own. If you use any "combining roots", add them to the "Other Roots" box. Try to think of an antonym and a synonym for each word you build.

www.DynamicLiteracy.com

157

My Word Wall

Root: *claim, clam, clat*

Word	Synonym / Antonym	Word	Synonym / Antonym

Morphemes for this meaning family

Prefixes	Roots	Suffixes

www.dynamicliteracy.com

Root Squares

How many words can you make?

Start in any square. Your goal is to combine two or more word parts to make as many words in the 'leg, lege, legis' family as you can. Write each word and the definition you can think of for it in the space provided at the bottom of the page. Use the back of the page if you need to.

al	ize	ate
il	leg, lege, legis	late
ive	ion	acy

Magic Squares

Name _____

Select the best answer for each of the words in the 'leg, lege, legis' family from the numbered definitions. Put the number in the proper space in the Magic Square box. If the total of the numbers is the same both across and down, you have found the magic number!

'leg, lege, legis' means law; bind in purpose

WORDS

A. allegedly
B. colleges
C. delegated
D. illegally
E. legacies
F. legalizing
G. legislating
H. privileges
I. legislator

DEFINITIONS

1. making lawful
2. acts of depriving things of their holy character; acts of desecrating things of their hol
3. a group sent away bound to a purpose; a group entrusted with an appointment
4. laws or rights belonging to individuals; unique benefits or honors
5. groups bound together to a purpose; institutions of higher learning
6. bringing into law; enacting law
7. in a manner addressing the law; so as to accuse without legal evidence
8. in a manner that is not lawful
9. sent away bound to a purpose; entrusted with an appointment
10. a statement toward the law; a claim without legal evidence
11. a person who brings into law; a person who enacts laws
12. legal gifts of personal property by will; things inherited

Magic Square Box

A.	B.	C.
D.	E.	F.
G.	H.	I.

Magic Number ____

www.dynamicliteracy.com

Stair Steps

Fill in the missing letters of each 'leg, lege, legis' word by using the definitions below
'leg, lege, legis' means law; bind in purpose

1.	l	e	g		

| 2. | | | l | e | g | e |

| 3. | | | l | e | g | |

| 4. | l | e | g | | |

| 5. | | | l | e | g |

| 6. | | | l | e | g |

| 7. | l | e | g | i | s |

| 8. | l | e | g | i | s |

1. lawful
2. to address the law; to accuse without legal evidence
3. not lawful
4. to make lawful
5. in a manner that is not lawful
6. a statement toward the law; a claim without legal evidence
7. a group that brings into law; a body that enacts laws
8. acts or processes of bringing into law; enactments of law

Being President

Becoming and being president is a tough job. While you're running for office, all sorts of ugly <u>claims made without evidence</u> are brought up against you and dirty tricks done to you. Your enemies might <u>make accusations</u> that you once got a speeding ticket or said bad words.

You have to win over most of the <u>people entrusted with an appointment</u> at the nominating convention. You need to be careful about which contributions are <u>lawful</u> and which ones are <u>not lawful</u>. Even if you persuade a majority of the people to vote for you, you still have to be elected by the electoral <u>group bound together for a purpose</u>.

If after all that, you do get elected, then you have to start worrying about keeping your power of executive <u>rights belonging to you individually</u> and planning your <u>lawful gift to be left behind</u> once you leave the position. You have to compromise with <u>law makers</u> who are there to check and balance you, and you have to try to get your favorite policies <u>brought into law</u>. It's hard work!

Fill in the blanks below using words from the "leg, lege, legis" family.

1. There have been serious _____ against some candidates.

2. One candidate was _____ to have insulted vegetarians by eating a burger.

3. States send _____ to a national convention which will nominate someone.

4. The size of contributions must stay within _____ limits; otherwise,

    _____ contributions can ruin a candidate.

5. The electoral _____ makes the ultimate decision about who wins.

6. Each branch of government has specific rights and _____.

7. Presidents think about the _____ that they will leave behind.

8. Members of the Senate and House, called _____, are meant to serve as a check on

    the president's power.

9. Presidents hope to have policies _____ which suit them.

Word Bank

allegations	delegates	legacy	legislators
alleged	illegal	legal	privileges
college	illegality	legislated	sacrilege

www.dynamicliteracy.com

Morpheme Mania

Prefixes
il al de col

leg, lege, legis
law; bind in purpose

Suffixes
al ate ize ion
s ive acy
er

Words & Definitions
legal - lawful

Synonyms
lawful

Antonyms
criminal

Roots
late

Other

Build as many words as you can for this root family. Use the prefixes and suffixes listed, or <u>add your own</u>. If you use any "combining roots", add them to the "Other Roots" box. Try to think of an antonym and a synonym for each word you build.

©2007 Dynamic Literacy, LLC

www.DynamicLiteracy.com

163

Root: *leg, lege, legis*

Word	Synonym / Antonym	Word	Synonym / Antonym

Morphemes for this meaning family

Prefixes	Roots	Suffixes

　　　www.dynamicliteracy.com

Root Squares

Name

How many words can you make?

Start in any square. Your goal is to combine two or more word parts to make as many words in the 'loc' family as you can. Write each word and the definition you can think of for it in the space provided at the bottom of the page. Use the back of the page if you need to.

al	ity	dis
mis	loc	re
ize	or	ate

　　　www.dynamicliteracy.com

Magic Squares

Select the best answer for each of the words in the 'loc' family from the numbered definitions. Put the number in the proper space in the Magic Square box. If the total of the numbers is the same both across and down, you have found the magic number!

'loc' means place

WORDS

A. allocation
B. dislocations
C. localities
D. locators
E. misallocated
F. localizing
G. relocate
H. dislocates
I. misallocations

DEFINITIONS

1. people or tools that find places
2. to place toward; to set aside or distribute
3. found in a certain place
4. places apart; moves out of usual or proper place
5. acts or processes of placing apart; movements out of the usual or proper place
6. acts of placing things toward badly; poor jobs setting aside or distributing
7. specific places
8. putting into or finding at a specific place
9. act of placing things toward; act of setting aside or distributing
10. finding in a place again; moving to a new place
11. to find in a place again; to move to a new place
12. placed things toward badly; did a poor job setting aside or distributing

Magic Square Box

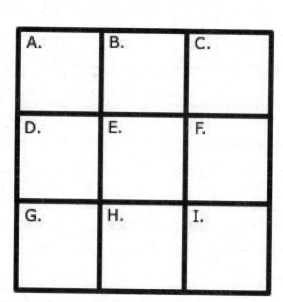

Magic Number _____

www.dynamicliteracy.com

Stair Steps

Name _____

Fill in the missing letters of each 'loc' word by using the definitions below
'loc' means place

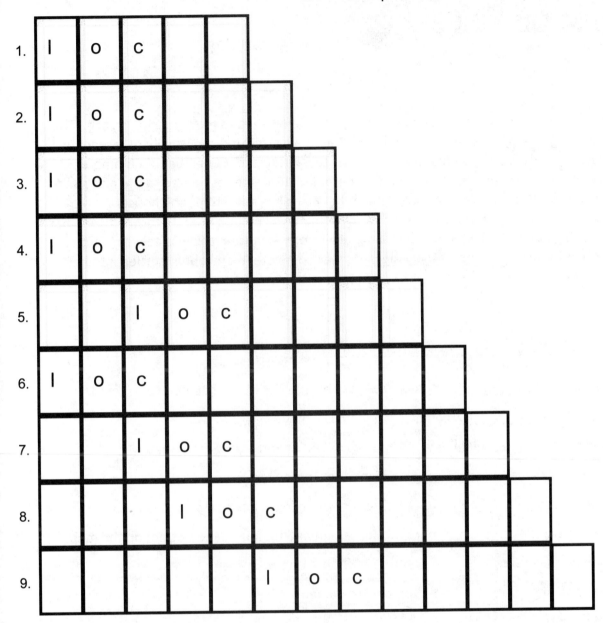

1. l o c

2. l o c

3. l o c

4. l o c

5. l o c

6. l o c

7. l o c

8. l o c

9. l o c

1. of a particular place
2. to find in a place
3. a person or tool that finds places
4. to put into or find at a specific place
5. found in a place again; moved to a new place
6. putting into or finding at a specific place
7. acts of placing things toward; acts of setting aside or distributing
8. acts or processes of placing apart; movements out of the usual or proper place
9. placing things toward badly; doing a poor job setting aside or distributing

www.dynamicliteracy.com

Moving Day

Jan's father earned a promotion in his job and the family had to <u>move to a new place</u>. The company <u>set aside for distribution</u> some money for the move but the responsibility of researching the new <u>specific places in a region</u> fell to Jan. She wrote a letter to the Chamber of Commerce in her new city and they sent her information on significant historic sites <u>as related to the place</u> and maps <u>of the specific place</u> so that she could <u>find in that place</u> her new street and house.

Once the moving truck was packed, Jan and her family piled into the SUV for the trip to her new house. Using directions and a map she had gotten from a website, she was able to find the <u>place</u> easily. Once the <u>act of moving to a new place</u> was completed, Jan happily settled into her new environment.

Fill in the blanks below using words from the "loc" family.

1. Jan's family had to _____ to a new city because her father had been promoted.

2. The company _____ money for the family's move.

3. Finding your way around in new _____ might be difficult without maps.

4. Historical sites that were _____ significant interested Jan.

5. Jan requested _____ maps of her new town to learn her new surroundings.

6. Before she could _____ her new house, Jan had to find the new street on the map.

7. Jan found the exact _____ of her new house on a web-map.

8. With so much information about her new town, Jan's _____ to a new environment went smoothly.

Word Bank

allocated	localities	location	relocate
dislocate	locally	locators	relocation
local	locate	misallocation	misallocating

Morpheme Mania

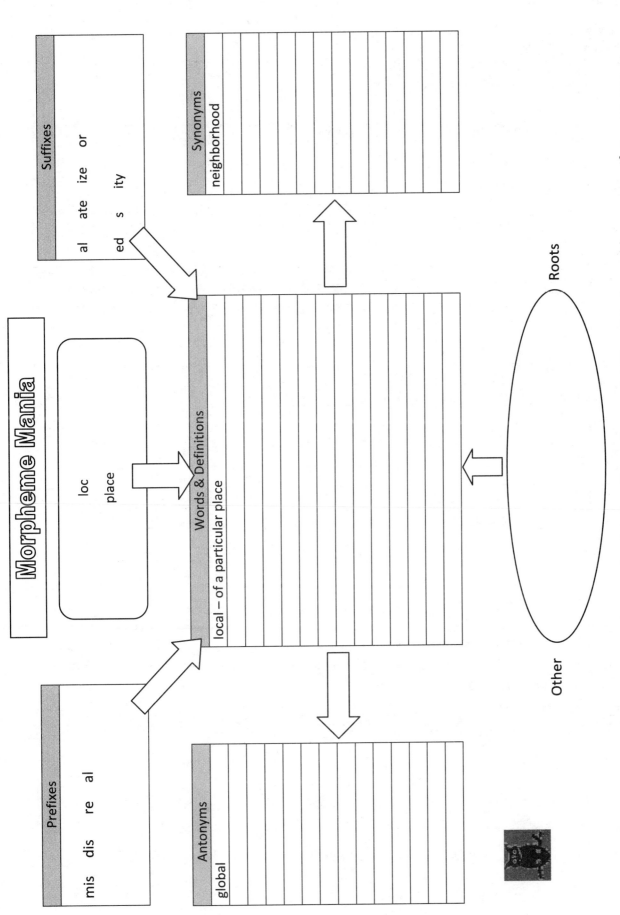

Prefixes

mis   dis   re   al

Suffixes

al   ate   ize   or

ed   s   ity

loc

place

Words & Definitions

local – of a particular place

Synonyms

neighborhood

Antonyms

global

Roots

Other

Build as many words as you can for this root family. Use the prefixes and suffixes listed, or add your own. If you use any "combining roots", add them to the "Other Roots" box. Try to think of an antonym and a synonym for each word you build.

My Word Wall

Root: *loc*

Word	Synonym / Antonym	Word	Synonym / Antonym

Morphemes for this meaning family

Prefixes	Roots	Suffixes

www.dynamicliteracy.com

Root Squares

How many words can you make?

Start in any square. Your goal is to combine two or more word parts to make as many words in the 'serv, serve' family as you can. Write each word and the definition you can think of for it in the space provided at the bottom of the page. Use the back of the page if you need to.

Name _____

at	ion	con
re	serv, serve	ory
pre	ist	ob

_____

_____

_____

_____

_____

_____

_____

_____

_____

_____

_____

www.dynamicliteracy.com

Magic Squares

Select the best answer for each of the words in the 'serv, serve' family from the numbered definitions. Put the number in the proper space in the Magic Square box. If the total of the numbers is the same both across and down, you have found the magic number!

'serv, serve' means to save or protect

WORDS	DEFINITIONS
A. conservationists	1. tending to watch over or keep safe
B. observational	2. related to watching over or keeping safe
C. reservations	3. people who watch over or keep safe; people who notice
D. preserver	4. a person who protects or saves thoroughly
E. observatory	5. saves or keeps back
F. conservatively	6. place for watching over or keeping safe; a planetarium
G. reserves	7. acts of saving or keeping back; hesitations
H. preservatives	8. in a manner that saves or protects thoroughly
I. observers	9. people who act to save or protect thoroughly
	10. substances serving to protect or save thoroughly

Magic Square Box

A.	B.	C.
D.	E.	F.
G.	H.	I.

Magic Number ____

Stair Steps

Name

Fill in the missing letters of each 'serv, serve' word by using the definitions below
'serv, serve' means to save or protect

1. | | | s | e | r | v | e | |
2. | | | | s | e | r | v | e |
3. | | | s | e | r | v | | |
4. | | | | s | e | r | v | |
5. | | | s | e | r | v | | |
6. | | | s | e | r | v | | |
7. | | | s | e | r | v | | |
8. | | | s | e | r | v | | |

1. to save or keep back
2. to protect or save thoroughly
3. saving or keeping back
4. saving or protecting thoroughly
5. an act of watching over or keeping safe
6. acts of saving or keeping back; hesitations
7. places for watching over or keeping safe; planetaria
8. in a manner that saves or protects thoroughly

www.dynamicliteracy.com

Lorenzo the Champion of Trees

Uncle Lorenzo was a good old character <u>who kept himself back</u> and who hardly ever said a word, except when it came to <u>the act of thoroughly protecting</u> natural resources, especially trees, or <u>the act of keeping as before</u> famous battlefields. He was an ardent <u>person who believed in thoroughly saving</u> and a <u>person believing in keeping as before</u>. He had no <u>acts of hesitation</u> about arguing with folks over the slow disappearance of trees and of open space, but on other issues, he <u>thoroughly saved</u> his energy. He kept an eye <u>tending to watch out</u> on land developers who weren't interested in <u>keeping safe</u> the land.

Throughout his hundred and one years, he always <u>kept</u> Arbor Day in honor of trees and Memorial Day in honor of soldiers.

Fill in the blanks below using words from the "serv, serve" family.

1. Lorenzo was a quiet, _____ old man.

2. However, he was vocal when it came to the _____ of natural resources.

3. He was also very interested in the _____ and upkeep of famous battle sites.

4. Lorenzo was an early _____ and _____ who inspired many to hold onto

   nature and history.

5. He had no _____ about making his anti-development viewpoints known.

6. On most other issues, though, he _____ his energy and kept quiet.

7. Lorenzo was a very _____ reader about land deals and new developments.

8. He knew that developers were not interested in _____ nature.

9. All his life Lorenzo_____ two holidays with special honor.

Word Bank

conservation	observant	preservation	preserve
conservationist	observed	preservationist	reserved
conserved	observances	preserving	reservations

www.dynamicliteracy.com

Morpheme Mania

Prefixes

pre   con   re   ob

serv, serve

to save or protect

Suffixes

at   ion   ory   ist

ed   s   er   ing

Words & Definitions

conserve – to save or protect thoroughly

Synonyms

save

Antonyms

waste

Roots

Other

Build as many words as you can for this root family. Use the prefixes and suffixes listed, or add your own. If you use any "combining roots", add them to the "Other Roots" box. Try to think of an antonym and a synonym for each word you build.

www.DynamicLiteracy.com

Root: *serv, serve*

Word	Synonym / Antonym	Word	Synonym / Antonym

Morphemes for this meaning family

Prefixes	Roots	Suffixes

www.dynamicliteracy.com

Root Squares

Name

How many words can you make?

Start in any square. Your goal is to combine two or more word parts to make as many words in the 'capit, cep, cip, cipit' family as you can. Write each word and the definition you can think of for it in the space provided at the bottom of the page. Use the back of the page if you need to.

de	al	tri
pre	capit, cep, cip, cipit	ate
ism	ize	ion

_____

_____

_____

_____

_____

_____

_____

_____

_____

_____

Magic Squares

Name _____

Select the best answer for each of the words in the 'capit, cep, cip, cipit' family from the numbered definitions. Put the number in the proper space in the Magic Square box. If the total of the numbers is the same both across and down, you have found the magic number!

'capit, cep, cip, cipit' means head; chief; wealth

WORDS

A. triceps
B. principals
C. precipitation
D. decapitates
E. capitalization
F. capitalist
G. capitalized
H. principality
I. biceps

DEFINITIONS

1. act of making the head letter of a word big; act of making an upper-case letter
2. the act of bowing one's head in defeat; the act giving up or surrendering
3. fell head-first; fell, as rain or snow from the sky
4. made the head or first letter of a word big; made an upper-case letter
5. things three-headed; three-massed muscles at the backs of the arms
6. things two-headed; muscles with two masses
7. act or process of falling head-first; a type of weather falling from the sky
8. a person whose focus is on wealth
9. the heads of or firsts among; major items; people in charge
10. to tell the head or main points again
11. state ruled by a head citizen; state ruled by a prince or chief
12. cuts off the head of a person or thing

Magic Square Box

A.	B.	C.
D.	E.	F.
G.	H.	I.

Magic Number ____

Stair Steps

Name

Fill in the missing letters of each 'capit, cep, cip, cipit' word by using the definitions below
'capit, cep, cip, cipit' means head; chief; wealth

1. | | | | c | e | p | | | | | | |

2. c | a | p | i | t | | |

3. c | a | p | i | t | | | |

4. | | | c | i | p | | | |

5. c | a | p | i | t | | | |

6. | | | c | i | p | | | | | |

7. | | c | a | p | i | t | | | | |

8. | | c | i | p | i | t | | | | |

9. c | a | p | i | t | | | | | | | |

1. something three-headed; a three-massed muscle at the back of the arm
2. the head seat of government; wealth; upper-case letter
3. the head seats of government; upper-case letters
4. the head of or first among; major item; the person in charge
5. belief based on wealth, originally heads of cattle; economic system advocating a free flow of wealth
6. mainly or chiefly
7. the act of cutting off the head
8. falling head-first; falling, as rain or snow from the sky
9. act of making the head letter of a word big; act of making an upper-case letter

www.dynamicliteracy.com

The Peasants Stage a Revolution

The starving peasants stormed into the country's <u>main city</u> and <u>chiefly</u> demanded that the cruel queen come to speak to them. She simply laughed at their demand and refused <u>to bow her head in defeat</u>. The <u>chief head</u> of the rebels stood up, flexed his <u>two-headed arm muscles</u>, and demanded that they <u>cut the head off</u> of the queen.

There was a hush for a moment, but then the leader <u>called out the main points</u> <u>again</u> and reminded them of their misery. His words caused a noisy riot to <u>fall head-first</u>, and the peasants rushed <u>head-long</u> into the palace, held a quick trial, and <u>cut off her head</u> and the heads of many of her attendants.

Fill in the blanks below using words from the "capit, cep, cip, cipit" family.

1. The queen resided in the _____ city of her country.

2. The people wanted foremost and _____ that the queen speak to them.

3. The proud queen refused to _____ to their demand.

4. The _____ leader of the rebellion was good at urging on the crowd.

5. The flexing of his _____ became a symbol of power for the people.

6. The bold call to _____ the queen caused shock at first in the mob.

7. The leader _____ the reasons they had come and pulled the mob out of their

   silence.

8. His reminders of their misery _____ a loud riot.

9. The peasants ran boldly and _____ into the palace.

10. In a short while, the queen and many others were _____.

Word Bank

biceps	capitalizing	decapitated	principal
capital	capitulate	precipitated	principally
capitalism	decapitate	precipitously	recapitulated

www.dynamicliteracy.com

Morpheme Mania

Prefixes

pre   tri   de   prin

re   bi

Suffixes

al   ate   ism   ize

ed   s   ul

capit, cep, cip, cipit

head; chief; wealth

Words & Definitions

capitalism – system based on wealth

Synonyms

competition

Antonyms

communism

Roots

Other

Build as many words as you can for this root family. Use the prefixes and suffixes listed, or add your own. If you use any "combining roots", add them to the "Other Roots" box. Try to think of an antonym and a synonym for each word you build.

My Word Wall

Name

Root: *capit, cep, cip, cipit*

Word	Synonym / Antonym	Word	Synonym / Antonym

Morphemes for this meaning family

Prefixes	Roots	Suffixes

Root Squares

How many words can you make?

Start in any square. Your goal is to combine two or more word parts to make as many words in the 'gener' family as you can. Write each word and the definition you can think of for it in the space provided at the bottom of the page. Use the back of the page if you need to.

ate	al	de
ic	gener	ize
re	ion	ous

_____

_____

_____

_____

_____

_____

_____

_____

_____

_____

_____

Magic Squares

Name _____

Select the best answer for each of the words in the 'gener' family from the numbered definitions. Put the number in the proper space in the Magic Square box. If the total of the numbers is the same both across and down, you have found the magic number!

'gener' means family, creation, birth, or sort

WORDS

A. degenerating
B. generality
C. generational
D. regeneration
E. generator
F. generosity
G. generic
H. generous
I. regenerate

DEFINITIONS

1. process of declining into a less desirable sort; act or process of deteriorating
2. statement involving most members of a group; a commonality
3. to produce one of the same sort again
4. act or process of producing one of the same sort again
5. of the same sort; without a brand name
6. a device or person that creates
7. belonging by birth to one group
8. quality of being of good "family" or breeding; quality of giving to others freely
9. declining into a less desirable sort; deteriorating
10. of good "family" or breeding; giving freely

Magic Square Box

A.	B.	C.
D.	E.	F.
G.	H.	I.

Magic Number _____

www.dynamicliteracy.com

Stair Steps

Name

Fill in the missing letters of each 'gener' word by using the definitions below
'gener' means family, creation, birth, or sort

1. | g | e | n | e | r | | | |
2. | g | e | n | e | r | | |
3. | g | e | n | e | r | | |
4. | g | e | n | e | r | |
5. | | | g | e | n | e | r |
6. | g | e | n | e | r |
7. | | g | e | n | e | r |
8. | g | e | n | e | r |

1. relating to many members of a group or family
2. to produce one of the same sort
3. in a manner relating to many members of a group; as a rule
4. as from of good "family" or breeding; in a manner giving freely
5. produced one of the same sort again
6. simplifying into one group or sort
7. processes of declining into a less desirable sort; acts or processes of deteriorating
8. an act of simplifying into one group or sort

www.dynamicliteracy.com

Nothing Really New

Every new <u>group born in the same era</u> seems to go through the same process. We are in our early years <u>as a rule</u> under the guidance of parents, but at some point in childhood we try to be different from them. The search for something new <u>produces</u> a sense that the previous values <u>belonging by birth to one group</u> are too old-fashioned. The parents see this as <u>a process of declining to a less desirable sort</u>, with unfamiliar <u>sorts</u> of music, clothing, and even language.

In time, the new takes the place of the old, and the same cycle begins all over. A new group is born and the search for the new and shocking is <u>produced again</u>. The new and shocking then becomes the standard <u>of the same sort</u>. Do you think it's too much of <u>an act of simplifying into one sort</u> to say that all the <u>groups born in the same era</u> have more in common with each other than they have differences?

Fill in the blanks below using words from the "gener" family.

1. It appears that every _____ goes through the same experiences.

2. _____ speaking, young people try to be different from their parents.

3. Peer pressure _____ a search for new values.

4. The _____ values seem old-fashioned to newcomers.

5. Parents often consider new values a _____ from what theirs are.

6. The new types or _____ of music, clothes, and language may disturb parents.

7. This cycle is _____ over and over.

8. _____ standards last for just a short while.

9. It may not be too much of a _____ to say that all groups are the same.

10. All _____ seem to have at least one common experience.

Word Bank

degeneration	generalization	generation	generic
genera	generally	generations	generosity
generalists	generates	generational	regenerated

www.dynamicliteracy.com

Morpheme Mania

Prefixes

re   de

Suffixes

al   ate   ic   ize

s   ist   ion   ous

gener

family, creation, birth, or sort

Words & Definitions

general – relating to many members of a family

Synonyms

widespread

Antonyms

specific

Roots

Other

Build as many words as you can for this root family. Use the prefixes and suffixes listed, or add your own. If you use any "combining roots", add them to the "Other Roots" box. Try to think of an antonym and a synonym for each word you build.

www.DynamicLiteracy.com

Name _____

Root: *gener*

Word	Synonym / Antonym	Word	Synonym / Antonym

Morphemes for this meaning family

Prefixes	Roots	Suffixes

Root Squares

How many words can you make?

Start in any square. Your goal is to combine two or more word parts to make as many words in the 'flex, flect' family as you can. Write each word and the definition you can think of for it in the space provided at the bottom of the page. Use the back of the page if you need to.

ity	or	ive
de	**flex, flect**	in
re	ed	ibil

www.dynamicliteracy.com

Magic Squares

Select the best answer for each of the words in the 'flex, flect' family from the numbered definitions. Put the number in the proper space in the Magic Square box. If the total of the numbers is the same both across and down, you have found the magic number!

'flex, flect' means to bend, turn, or change direction

WORDS
A. deflected
B. flex
C. flexibly
D. inflectional
E. reflexive
F. reflections
G. reflector
H. inflexibility
I. reflectedly

DEFINITIONS
1. quality of not being able to bend or change; rigidity
2. related to bending or turning into; related to changing words into their other forms
3. in a manner able to bend
4. things bent or turned back; acts of glancing back at or pondering
5. to bend; to bend a joint or contract a muscle
6. a surface that bends or turns back; something that directs back light
7. bent away; redirected
8. in a manner bent or turned back; so as to glance back at or ponder
9. turned back on itself; responded instinctively on itself

Magic Square Box

A.	B.	C.
D.	E.	F.
G.	H.	I.

Magic Number ____

www.dynamicliteracy.com

Stair Steps

Name

Fill in the missing letters of each 'flex, flect' word by using the definitions below
'flex, flect' means to bend, turn, or change direction

1. | f | l | e | x | | |

2. | | | f | l | e | c | t |

3. | | | f | l | e | x |

4. | | | f | l | e | x |

5. | | | f | l | e | c | t |

6. | f | l | e | x |

7. | | | f | l | e | c | t |

8. | f | l | e | x |

9. | | | f | l | e | c | t |

1. bent; bent a joint or tensed a muscle
2. to bend or turn back; to glance back at or ponder
3. acts of bending or turning back; acts of instinctively responding
4. turned back on itself; responded instinctively on itself
5. things that cause to bend away
6. quality of being able to bend
7. related to bending or turning into; related to changing words into their other forms
8. qualities of being able to bend
9. so as to bend or change into; so as to change words into their other forms

www.dynamicliteracy.com

"Kneesworthy" Advice

Take care of your knees! Your knees take care of you. Just <u>glance back</u> for a moment on how much stress your knees take each day, with every step you take, especially if you are a runner. To keep your knees healthy, be sure to <u>bend</u> them often, so that they stay <u>bendable</u>.

Actually, what <u>bends</u> the knee or any joint is a muscle called a <u>thing that bends</u>. By exercising such muscles you avoid <u>the quality of not being able to bend</u> and pain in the joints. Check the <u>instinctive bending response</u> in your knees with a tap; good <u>quality of being able to bend</u> in your knees helps you run from a dangerous situation. If you run in the evenings, be sure to wear <u>things that bend light back</u> on your clothing so you can <u>redirect</u> traffic away from you.

Fill in the blanks below using words from the "flex, flect" family.

1. We should often _____ on how to maintain healthy bones and muscles.

2. You should _____ your knees and elbows often to keep them limber.

3. _____ joints tend to be pain-free.

4. A specific muscle _____ each joint.

5. A muscle that helps bend a joint is called a _____.

6. _____ in a joint causes swelling and pain.

7. Healthy knees have an automatic kicking _____ when they are tapped.

8. Joint _____ can save your life.

9. Wear _____ if you are walking or running after dark.

10. You want to be able to _____ traffic away from you.

Word Bank

deflect	flexibility	inflexibility	reflections
flex	flexible	reflectors	reflex
flexes	flexor	reflect	reflexive

www.dynamicliteracy.com

Morpheme Mania

Prefixes

re   de   in

Suffixes

or   ity   ed   ive

s   ibil   ion

flex, flect

to bend, turn, or change direction

Words & Definitions

reflect – to bend or turn back

Synonyms

return

Antonyms

absorb

Other   Roots

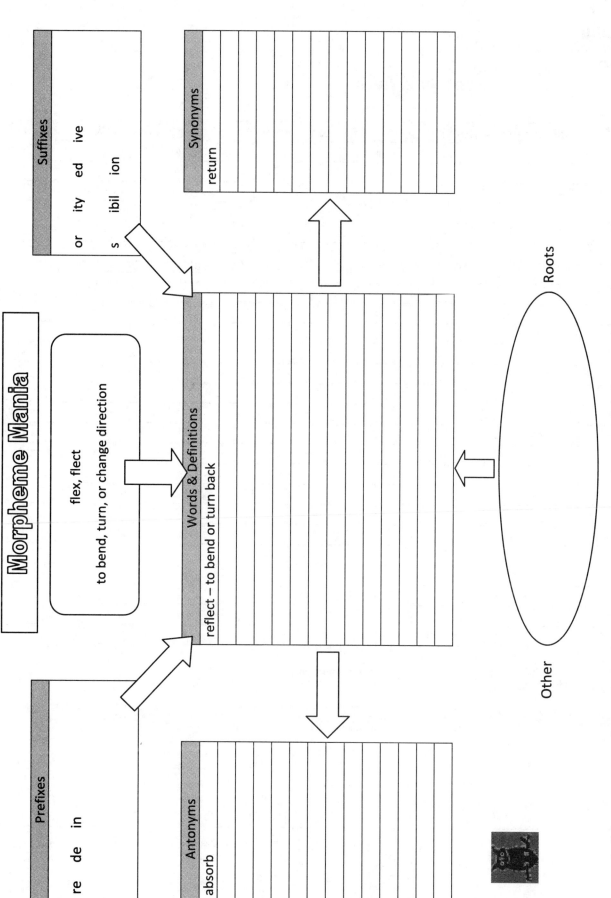

Build as many words as you can for this root family. Use the prefixes and suffixes listed, or add your own. If you use any "combining roots", add them to the "Other Roots" box. Try to think of an antonym and a synonym for each word you build.

www.DynamicLiteracy.com

My Word Wall

Name

Root: *flex, flect*

Word	Synonym / Antonym	Word	Synonym / Antonym

Morphemes for this meaning family

Prefixes	Roots	Suffixes

www.dynamicliteracy.com

Root Squares

How many words can you make?

Start in any square. Your goal is to combine two or more word parts to make as many words in the 'sect, secti, sec, seg' family as you can. Write each word and the definition you can think of for it in the space provided at the bottom of the page. Use the back of the page if you need to.

bi	or	dis
inter	**sect, secti, sec, seg**	in
ion	ment	al

    www.dynamicliteracy.com

Magic Squares

Select the best answer for each of the words in the 'sect, secti, sec, seg' family from the numbered definitions. Put the number in the proper space in the Magic Square box. If the total of the numbers is the same both across and down, you have found the magic number!

'sect, secti, sec, seg' means to cut, divide

WORDS

A. bisected
B. dissecting
C. insects
D. intersected
E. sectarian
F. sectionalism
G. segments
H. sections
I. intersectional

DEFINITIONS

1. agent that kills animals with incut bodies; agent that exterminates bugs
2. cutting apart; analyzing
3. relating to places cut into by each other; pertaining to a crossroad
4. cut in between; crossed
5. pieces cut off from other things
6. a person belonging to a group cut from a larger group; a member of a cult
7. animals whose body shapes are cut inward; bugs
8. preference for a small area cut from a larger area; a partiality for some particular pla
9. cut into two halves
10. pieces cut from the whole; segments

Magic Square Box

A.	B.	C.
D.	E.	F.
G.	H.	I.

Magic Number ____

Stair Steps

Name

Fill in the missing letters of each 'sect, secti, sec, seg' word by using the definitions below
'sect, secti, sec, seg' means to cut, divide

1. | s | e | c | t | | |
2. | | | s | e | c | t | |
3. | s | e | g | | | | |
4. | | | s | e | c | t | | |
5. | | | | | s | e | c | t | |
6. | | | | s | e | c | t | | | |
7. | | | s | e | c | t | i | | | | |
8. | s | e | c | t | | | | | | | |
9. | | | | | s | e | c | t | | | | | |

1. an area cut from a bigger area; a precinct
2. cuts into two parts
3. pieces cut off from other things
4. instruments that cut into halves
5. cuts in between; crosses
6. acts of cutting apart; separations acts of analysis
7. agents that kill animals with incut bodies; bug poisons
8. people who prefer small areas cut from larger areas; people partial to local interests & customs
9. relating to places cut into by each other; pertaining to a crossroad

www.dynamicliteracy.com

The Father of Entomology

William Kirby, an English minister, was opposed to Thomas Paine and other <u>people who believed in cutting off an area</u> from the British Empire. He did not want to see America <u>cut as a smaller area</u> from England, but the American Revolution settled that debate.

Yet William Kirby is more famous for something else. Open a science book and turn to the <u>part cut off from the rest</u> concerning biology, where you might find something about him. He is known for his studies of the <u>little animals with bodies that seem cut inward</u>, especially bees. In bees he believed that he saw the <u>point at which</u> religion and nature <u>cut into each other</u>. He did not approve of poisonous <u>agents that kill these in-cut creatures</u>, but he nevertheless advanced our knowledge by <u>cutting apart</u> their bodies and discovering their three <u>pieces that seem cut</u>.

After the <u>acts of cutting apart</u> and analyzing, Kirby drew pictures and wrote studies that became, in 1815, the first popular book on the subject in English.

Fill in the blanks below using words from the "sect, secti, sec, seg" family.

1. Thomas Paine and many American colonists were _____; they wanted America to break off from the larger Empire.

2. The broken and _____ Empire bothered William Kirby, but he turned his attention to new things.

3. You may learn about William Kirby in the biology _____ of a science book.

4. He studied _____ such as bees.

5. He believed that bees were an example of the _____ of Nature and religious teachings.

6. He did not approve of using poisonous _____ .

7. Kirby is famous for _____ bees and examining their bodies.

8. The bodies of bees and animals like them have three _____.

9. From his _____ Kirby compiled an important and popular study on Entomology.

Word Bank

bisects	insects	section	sectors
dissecting	insecticides	sectional	segmented
dissections	intersection	sectionalists	segments

www.dynamicliteracy.com

Morpheme Mania

Prefixes

bi dis in inter

sect, secti, sec, seg

to cut, divide

Suffixes

al ion ment s

ed ing arian

Words & Definitions

section – a piece cut from the whole

Synonyms

chunk

Antonyms

whole

Roots

cide

Other

Build as many words as you can for this root family. Use the prefixes and suffixes listed, or add your own. If you use any "combining roots", add them to the "Other Roots" box. Try to think of an antonym and a synonym for each word you build.

www.DynamicLiteracy.com

My Word Wall

Root: *sect, secti, sec, seg*

Word	Synonym / Antonym	Word	Synonym / Antonym

Morphemes for this meaning family

Prefixes	Roots	Suffixes

www.dynamicliteracy.com

Root Squares

How many words can you make?

Start in any square. Your goal is to combine two or more word parts to make as many words in the 'par, pare, pair' family as you can. Write each word and the definition you can think of for it in the space provided at the bottom of the page. Use the back of the page if you need to.

ir	ate	pre
able	par, pare, pair	ion
se	ory	re

_____

_____

_____

_____

_____

_____

_____

_____

_____

_____

_____

www.dynamicliteracy.com

Magic Squares

Name

Select the best answer for each of the words in the 'par, pare, pair' family from the numbered definitions. Put the number in the proper space in the Magic Square box. If the total of the numbers is the same both across and down, you have found the magic number!

'par, pare, pair' means arrange, order, command

WORDS	DEFINITIONS
A. inseparable	1. in a manner arranged or ordered apart; in a manner done apart from another
B. paraded	2. clothing arranged or laid out for an occasion
C. unseparated	3. arranged or trimmed for better appearance; cut into small pieces
D. separately	4. not able to be mended back into proper order
E. preparations	5. moved forward in a formal arrangement for show; processed along in a line
F. repairable	6. object arranged for preparing to do a task; a device for a particular purpose
G. preparatory	7. not arranged or ordered apart; together, not parted
H. irreparable	8. able to be arranged back into proper order; fixable
I. apparatus	9. not able to be arranged or moved apart
	10. not having arranged things beforehand; not ready
	11. tending to arrange a situation beforehand; serving to get things ready
	12. acts of putting in order or arranging beforehand; things done to get ready

Magic Square Box

A.	B.	C.
D.	E.	F.
G.	H.	I.

Magic Number ____

www.dynamicliteracy.com

Stair Steps

Name

Fill in the missing letters of each 'par, pare, pair' word by using the definitions below
'par, pare, pair' means arrange, order, command

1. | | | p | a | i | r | | |
2. | p | a | r | | | | |
3. | | | p | a | r | e | |
4. | | p | a | r | | | |
5. | | p | a | i | r | | |
6. | | p | a | r | | |
7. | | p | a | r | | |
8. | | | p | a | r | | |
9. | | | p | a | r | | | |

1. to arrange back into proper order; fix
2. moved forward in a formal arrangement for show; processed along in a line
3. to arrange beforehand; to get ready
4. to arrange or order apart; to part
5. arranging back into proper order; fixing
6. arranges or orders apart; takes things apart or moves apart
7. act of arranging or ordering apart; act of parting
8. not able to be mended back into proper order
9. acts of putting in order or arranging beforehand; things done to get ready

www.dynamicliteracy.com

Some Advice on Career Choices

The <u>process of getting ready</u> for a future choice of career doesn't mean you have to decide early what you'd like to do for a living. The good <u>person who arranges beforehand</u> for the future makes plans with diversity in mind. Try not to <u>arrange</u> yourself <u>apart</u> from opportunities to learn new things, whether it's learning <u>to arrange back into shape</u> faulty machinery, to design <u>clothing arranged for occasions</u>, or to stock scientific <u>devices for particular purposes</u>. Such <u>act of arranging yourself apart</u> leads to harm <u>not able to be put back in proper order</u> to your flexibility and job-holding potential.

Take as many classes <u>serving to get things ready</u> as you can in school. That way you will be happily <u>ready</u> to follow a variety of interests.

Fill in the blanks below using words from the "par, pare, pair" family.

1. _____ for future careers doesn't mean making final decisions now.

2. A person who is a good _____ for the future thinks about diversity.

3. Don't _____ yourself from offered opportunities.

4. There will always be broken machinery to _____.

5. People are always interested in nice wearing _____.

6. Science labs need certain _____ to carry out experiments.

7. _____ from opportunity leads to inflexibility.

8. Inflexibility can bring _____ harm to your attraction to employers.

9. A variety of _____ classes taken in school will provide future choices.

10. You will find yourself happily _____ for your chosen career.

Word Bank

apparatus	parade	prepared	separate
apparel	preparation	preparer	separation
irreparable	preparatory	repair	unprepared

www.dynamicliteracy.com

Morpheme Mania

Prefixes

re pre ir se

in un

par, pare, pair

arrange, order, command

Suffixes

ate ion able s

ed ory er

Words & Definitions

repaired – arranged back in proper order

Synonyms

fixed

Antonyms

broke

Roots

Other

Build as many words as you can for this root family. Use the prefixes and suffixes listed, or add your own. If you use any "combining roots", add them to the "Other Roots" box. Try to think of an antonym and a synonym for each word you build.

www.DynamicLiteracy.com

My Word Wall

Name _____

Root: *par, pare, pair*

Word	Synonym / Antonym	Word	Synonym / Antonym

Morphemes for this meaning family

Prefixes	Roots	Suffixes

www.dynamicliteracy.com

Root Squares

How many words can you make?

Start in any square. Your goal is to combine two or more word parts to make as many words in the 'via, vi, vey, voy' family as you can. Write each word and the definition you can think of for it in the space provided at the bottom of the page. Use the back of the page if you need to.

de	age	ob
pre	via, vi, vey, voy	con
ate	per	ous

_____

_____

_____

_____

_____

_____

_____

_____

_____

_____

_____

Magic Squares

Name _____

Select the best answer for each of the words in the 'via, vi, vey, voy' family from the numbered definitions. Put the number in the proper space in the Magic Square box. If the total of the numbers is the same both across and down, you have found the magic number!

'via, vi, vey, voy' means road, passageway, trip; to pass

WORDS	DEFINITIONS
A. conveyable	1. a person sent on a diplomatic trip
B. deviating	2. passes along with; makes known
C. deviously	3. a group of vehicles traveling together on a trip
D. conveys	4. in a manner being on the same passage but earlier; before
E. impervious	5. going on a trip
F. obviously	6. in a manner acting off from the road; in a meandering or scheming manner
G. voyaged	7. quality of being in the way of; quality of being evident
H. obviousness	8. going off from the road; straying from
I. voyaging	9. not allowing passage through; resistant to
	10. able to be passed along with; able to be made known
	11. related to the three basic roads to knowledge; related to something of small importan
	12. went on a trip
	13. in a manner in the way of; evidently

Magic Square Box

A.	B.	C.
D.	E.	F.
G.	H.	I.

Magic Number ____

Stair Steps

Fill in the missing letters of each 'via, vi, vey, voy' word by using the definitions below
'via, vi, vey, voy' means road, passageway, trip; to pass

			v	e	y				
1.			v	e	y				
2.	v	o	y						
3.		v	i						
4.			v	i					
5.	v	o	y						
6.		v	i						
7.			v	e	y				
8.		v	i						
9.			v	e	y				

1. to pass along with; to make known
2. a trip
3. in the way of; evident
4. on the same passage at an earlier time; earlier
5. people who go on trips
6. in a manner in the way of; evidently
7. a means to pass along with; act of making known
8. acts of going off from the road; acts of straying from
9. various means to pass along with; acts of making known

www.dynamicliteracy.com

Caesar Blocks Swiss Plans

Caesar had just returned from a sea <u>trip</u> when he learned that the Swiss wanted to move as a group from their mountainous homeland to the coast <u>by way of</u> Roman territory. The Swiss sent <u>a person on the trip</u> to ask Caesar if that would be allowed.

Caesar <u>passed news along</u> to the Swiss messenger that he would decide about the issue soon. In reality, Caesar was acting rather <u>off the road and scheming</u>. He remembered that <u>on the same passage at an earlier time</u> there had been trouble with these same people.

With astonishing speed, Caesar marched an army with a big <u>group of vehicles traveling together</u> through the mountains toward the Swiss. He then ordered that a wall <u>which would not allow passage through</u> be built.

Then Caesar told the Swiss that he would not <u>go off the path</u> of Roman tradition by allowing them to pass through their property. He had <u>schemingly</u> bought time to be able to block the Swiss plan.

Fill in the blanks below using words from the "via, vi, vey, voy" family.

1. At the beginning of this story, Caesar had just returned from a _____.

2. He learned that the Swiss were heading toward the seacoast _____ Roman territory.

3. The Swiss sent an _____ to ask Caesar's permission.

4. Caesar _____ to him the message that he would think about it for a while.

5. Yet Caesar was being _____ with his message.

6. He recalled that _____ he had had trouble in this area.

7. He therefore gathered a big army with wagons and horses and quickly moved this

   _____ toward the area.

8. When he got there, he ordered an _____ barrier to be built to stop the Swiss.

9. It was only then that Caesar sent word to the Swiss that he would not _____ from

   Roman tradition by allowing the Swiss to enter Roman land.

10. Caesar had _____ stalled for time and was able to prevent the Swiss from moving.

Word Bank

conveyances	deviate	deviously	previously
conveyed	deviation	envoy	via
convoy	devious	impervious	voyage

www.dynamicliteracy.com

Morpheme Mania

Prefixes

de	pre	per	con
ob	en	tri	

Suffixes

ate	age	ous	s
al	ing	er	ed

via, vi, vey, voy

road, passageway, trip; to pass

Words & Definitions

deviate – to go off from the road

Synonyms

stray

Antonyms

confirm

Roots

Other

Build as many words as you can for this root family. Use the prefixes and suffixes listed, or add your own. If you use any "combining roots", add them to the "Other Roots" box. Try to think of an antonym and a synonym for each word you build.

All rights reserved

www.DynamicLiteracy.com

My Word Wall

Name _____

Root: *via, vi, vey, voy*

Word	Synonym / Antonym	Word	Synonym / Antonym

Morphemes for this meaning family

Prefixes	Roots	Suffixes

Root Squares

Name

How many words can you make?

Start in any square. Your goal is to combine two or more word parts to make as many words in the 'her, here, hes' family as you can. Write each word and the definition you can think of for it in the space provided at the bottom of the page. Use the back of the page if you need to.

ive	ion	in
ent	her, here, hes	co
ad	ence	ly

www.dynamicliteracy.com

Magic Squares

Name

Select the best answer for each of the words in the 'her, here, hes' family from the numbered definitions. Put the number in the proper space in the Magic Square box. If the total of the numbers is the same both across and down, you have found the magic number!

'her, here, hes' means to stick or cling

WORDS	DEFINITIONS
A. adhere	1. not tending to cling; not slow or reluctant to act
B. cohesions	2. things that stick to other things; types of glue or tape
C. adhesives	3. having the quality of sticking within; intrinsic or inborn
D. incohesive	4. state of not sticking together; quality of lacking sense or logic
E. incoherence	5. quality of sticking or clinging to
F. hesitantly	6. in a clinging manner; in a manner slow or reluctant to act
G. inherent	7. to stick to or cling to
H. adherence	8. tending not to stick together
I. coherences	9. processes of sticking together
	10. processes or acts of sticking together

Magic Square Box

A.	B.	C.
D.	E.	F.
G.	H.	I.

Magic Number ____

www.dynamicliteracy.com

Stair Steps

Fill in the missing letters of each 'her, here, hes' word by using the definitions below
'her, here, hes' means to stick or cling

1.   h   e   r   e
2.   h   e   r
3.   h   e   r
4.   h   e   r
5.   h   e   r
6. h   e   s
7.   h   e   r
8.   h   e   r

1. to stick together; to fit together
2. stuck to or clung to
3. sticking together
4. people who stick to a cause or belief; supporters or advocates
5. in the manner of sticking together; logically and sensibly
6. conditions of clinging; states of being slow or reluctant to act
7. in a manner not sticking together; so as to lack sense or logic
8. states of not sticking together; qualities of lacking sense or logic

The Failure That Wasn't

Sometimes a failure turns out to be a success. A man named Spencer was trying in 1970 to invent a super-strong <u>substance to stick to other things</u>. However, he came up with a substance that would <u>stick to things</u> all right, but did not have a permanent <u>state of sticking together</u>. He was <u>slow</u> to tell anyone about his failure, but he did tell his friend Art, hoping that there might be some usefulness <u>sticking within</u> about the product.

Four years later, Art was having trouble keeping up with all the passages he wanted to refer to in a book, since his bookmarkers kept falling out. He remembered Spencer's weak glue, was <u>not slow</u> about rubbing some of it on the markers, and the *Post-It* note was invented!

Just remember, the next time something seems <u>in an inborn manner</u> <u>making no sense or logic</u>, it may turn out to be a brilliant discovery.

Fill in the blanks below using words from the "her, here, hes" family.

1. Spencer was trying to develop a super-strong _____.

2. What he found did indeed _____ to things.

3. However, its quality of _____ was weak and temporary.

4. People are _____ to tell others about their mistakes or failures.

5. Many things that seem useless have some _____ value.

6. With inspiration, Art was _____ to try the new product in a new way.

7. The failure was actually not _____ a failure after all.

8. Things that make no sense or are _____ are often brilliant.

Word Bank

adhere	cohesion	hesitation	inherent
adherence	hesitant	incoherently	inherently
adhesive	hesitated	incoherent	unhesitant

www.dynamicliteracy.com

Morpheme Mania

Prefixes
in   co   ad

Suffixes
ive   ion   ent   s

ly   ed   ence

her, here, hes

to stick or cling

Words & Definitions
cohesive – tending to stick together

Synonyms
bound

Antonyms
scattered

Other

Roots

Build as many words as you can for this root family. Use the prefixes and suffixes listed, or add your own. If you use any "combining roots", add them to the "Other Roots" box. Try to think of an antonym and a synonym for each word you build.

©2007 Dynamic Literacy, LLC

www.DynamicLiteracy.com

217

My Word Wall

Name _____

Root: *her, here, hes*

Word	Synonym / Antonym	Word	Synonym / Antonym

Morphemes for this meaning family

Prefixes	Roots	Suffixes

NOTES

www.dynamicliteracy.com

www.dynamicliteracy.com